Wings OF TIME

Wings OF TIME

R.S. Haspiel

Library of Congress Control Number: 2021909871

HARDBACK: 978-1-955347-61-7
PAPERBACK: 978-1-955347-60-0
EBOOK: 978-1-955347-62-4

Ordering Information:

For orders and inquiries, please contact:
1-888-404-1388
www.goldtouchpress.com
book.orders@goldtouchpress.com

Printed in the United States of America

This book is dedicated to **my mom for the values and love she instilled in me and to my partner Marie who without her encouragement this book would have sat in its folder for another 10 years.**

PREFACE

I can remember seeing photographs of my mom in her 20's acting like a class clown with her female friends. If someone had told me my mom had a funny side, I would not have believed them. That picture was worth a thousand words. My mom would tell me of the times when she would paint live models at the Cochran Gallery in Washington, D.C. She also showed me black & white photographs of the generals she worked for when she was an Executive Secretary at the Pentagon. The phrase *"Loose Lips Sink Ships"* was a phrase that was well known in my household. Anytime I had a question she didn't wish to answer… out popped that phrase. In that respect she was a typical Jewish mother. My grandmother, of whom I rarely communicated with was Russian although Polish heritage was less threatening and got you into the states faster than being labeled a Russian. Ironic how the persecution was the same for both labels. I wasn't one who had a head for languages so I didn't catch on when trying to be taught Hebrew, Yiddish, German or Russian all of which my mother and grandmother spoke fluently. Since only my mom spoke English it made it difficult to communicate with my Russian/Polish grandmother.

I always wondered about the war that my parents and grandparents lived thru. When I would ask my mom, she would show me pictures of a General Arnold of whom she knew as an Executive Secretary in the Pentagon. When she mentioned a program and a group of women pilots called WASP's, she would always mention how capable and remarkable they were. I had often wondered why very little was ever mentioned within my high school textbooks of women pilots during the war. When I entered college in the 80's, it was still difficult to find any information of women and World War II. But as time passed, women grew stronger and with confidence from groups like the "Me Too" movement and "Times Up" more women from various countries were getting the courage to speak up. When continuing my research, I found out that around 800,000 women served in the Soviet Armed Forces. They constituted about 8% of the total Soviet military by the end of 1943. They mastered almost every military specialty. Over 100,000 women trained as snipers and some qualified as machine gunners.[1] While the American women served in the military during WWII their rank was never official, yet nurses served under combat conditions especially in the Philippines. American women flew planes both new, repaired and test to various destinations overseas but again were never in a combat capacity unlike the Night Witches of Russia.[2]

Once I began traveling, I realized there was more than one way to research. When I was in Washington, D.C. for a college fieldtrip I went to the National Archives and there, thanks to President Obama, were displays of women during WWII that were finally given the recognition and official rank they were due. Women such as Annie Fox who was the first woman to receive a Purple Heart and Reba Z. Whittle who was a prisoner of war after her aircraft was shot down in 1944. How about women like Elaine Row, Mary Roberts and Ellen Ainsworth who were the first women to be awarded the Silver Star. For those readers

---

[1] Z.M. Smimova-Medvedeva, On the Road To Stalingrad, Memoirs of a Woman Machine Gunner, Translator Introduction by Kazimiera J. Cottam.

[2] German nickname for a group of Russian women from the 588th Bomber Regiment. They would idle the engine near the target and glide to the area to be bombed. With only wind noise to reveal their location, the German soldiers said it sounded like broomsticks and named the pilots Night Witches.

who are of a younger generation the Silver Star was awarded for gallantry in action against an enemy of the United States. It's the Armed Forces 3rd highest decoration of valor in combat. Women like Ruby Bradley who was a prisoner of war and was awarded the Bronze Star (heroic service in a combat zone) long after WWII. Women who held the same rank as men during the war never were allowed the same recognition. We won't even mention the Russian women such as Lilya Litvayak and Katya Budanova who were the highest scoring flying aces in the Russian military or the famous Night Witches who flew night missions in wooden PO-2 planes during WWII.[3] What was even more interesting is that due to the weight of the bombs these planes carried and their low altitude, pilots didn't wear parachutes until 1944. Thirty-eight WASP died in WWII and all were fairly young women in their 20's and 30's. Three of those women were from the original WAFS.[4]

This book, even though it is a fictional account of two women during and after WWII, is dedicated to my mother and those other unmentioned women of the military. Their bravery and dedication of service during World War II, whether they were in the Philippines, Russia, Europe or United States are facts that should be in textbooks and taught in schools for generations to come. Lest we ignore the quote, **"Those who cannot remember the past are condemned to repeat it."**[5]

3

4   Jean Hascall Cole, Women Pilots of World War II

5   George Santayana, The Life of Reason, Volume I (1863-1952)

CHAPTER I

Dark clouds gathered over the rocky coastline as the car weaved its way around the curves of the not so traveled road. The sudden line of trees was in harsh contrast to the oceanside. It was a dreary, rainy November day when Katherine arrived at her grandmother's house in the country. Since she was 5 years old, she had been spending her vacations at her memaw's but now that she was 27 years old, she could think of a lot of other places she would like to be. Katherine's grandmother always seemed to be in another world. Her slight Russian accent always made Katherine curious about her grandmother's past but no one including Katherine's mom would discuss the past. Other than a slight Russian accent and her grandmothers first name being Natalya, Katherine knew virtually nothing about her grandmother other than she was a wonderful cook and was one of the few family members that would listen to her when she had something to say. One of the few bright sides to her visit was her grandmothers dog Barkley. Far from a usual dog, Barkley was a 120lb. Irish Wolfhound. Since it was summer, Katherine would fly to stay with her grandmother for the vacation. Barkley was usually left with friends while Katherine's grandmother made the long drive to pick her up. Katherine decided that today she would explore her grandmother's home more carefully until Barkley's return. Looking for clues that presented a better picture of her family's past…or so she hoped.

"Come child…I'm going to make us a nice salad from the garden."

Gardening was Memaw's specialty and seemed to give her great pleasure as she spent it coaxing blooms from errant young Basil plants.

"I'm tired Me maw. Can't I just walk around for a while?"

"Suit yourself my child. I will expect you at lunch time then."

Katherine was happy that she won that battle. Had her mother been here she probably wouldn't have said a word. With her usual stubborn air Katherine's grandmother tottered out the door. Katherine really wasn't tired but she was bored. Bored of the silence that being out in the country brought. She changed into a pair of comfortable blue jeans and began to explore her grandmothers two story cottage. A tiny room at the foot of the stairs seemed the logical place to start. As she climbed the stairs, she thought of those old classic horror films she use to watch with her mom. The ones where monsters lurked behind doors at the top of stairs. Stopping at the door she drew in a deep breath and slowly turned the door knob. Dusty sunlight filtered in from an Octagonal stain glass window as Katherine peered cautiously around the door. The small oblong room was filled with odd pieces of furniture, picture frames and several large antique chests. As she closed the door behind her she was startled by a sewing mannequin that seemed strategically placed behind the door. Katherine wished she could open up one of the windows as she smelled the stale musty air. She propped open the door slightly as she set about the room.

Katherine cautiously moved about the room taking in the strange assortment of items that seemed to have been collected over the years and stored with great care. As she moved several blankets, she noticed a large brown chest with a lock she had never seen before. When she lifted it up to take a closer look it clicked open. Katherine carefully removed the lock and set it down next to the blankets. She felt like a pirate about to discover a treasure. What she couldn't realize was that she was about to uncover so much more. The old chest creaked as she slowly opened the lid. The smell of old paper and a slight Lavender scent came from the chest as she opened it. As she looked down, she saw that the chest was full of different items carefully grouped together along with a folded military cap and what looked like a really cool bomber jacket with several patches sewed onto it. She removed the jacket assuming it was her grandfathers. But as she looked closer the wings on the patches were in Russian. She smiled as she recalled her grandfather complaining that he could never understand his wife when she got angry since he didn't speak Russian. She took a quick photo of it with her phone and set the jacket next to the blankets. To the left of the space where the jacket was were several bundles of what appeared to be neatly tied letters. Some were addressed to a barracks and some were addressed to her grandmother's old address in Britain. All were addressed to her grandmother's maiden name of Ritenkoph. She noticed how carefully the silk ribbon was tied. Some letters were stained and looked as though they had been thru a war. The Lavender scent she then realized was coming from the letters. She smiled as she thought of her grandmother having a war romance with a handsome young soldier boy that may or may not have been her grandfather. Although her mother's memory of her grandfather was kind and thoughtful, she also remembers her mother's comment about his frequent temper and how she assumed that the war made him that way. Her mother never liked how he treated her grandmother and always seemed to stop short of saying she was glad he died in the war. While in some ways Katherine missed having a grandfather both her mother and grandmother seemed happier when he wasn't mentioned. She picked up a stack of letters dated 1939. She moved an old thick cushion into the path of the filtered light and settled in. Katherine carefully untied the bow and gingerly opened the first Lavender scented envelope.

Dear Natalya,   August 31, 1939

Hope this letter finds you well. It seems like nursing school has been a blur compared to the talk of war which everyone here seems to think about. I miss our days of sitting in the courtyard as you read poetry. I loved having those banana sandwiches that you hated. Mrs. Simon was out yesterday tending to her Victory Garden as she called it. I have to admit this talk of war makes me nervous. Although I look forward to being of service in the London hospital, I have to admit your flight school sounds much more exciting. I know you were heading back down to France so I hope since you are on the move that you will write me at the hospital. By the time this letter finds you I should already be established there.

Love,
Emily

Katherine was puzzled by the letter as she re-read the part about her grandmother going to flight school. She remembered her mother mentioning a long time ago when her mother flew planes. But she never really mentioned the type of planes or where she learned to fly. Eager to learn more Katherine looked at the dates of the letters. She decided to open up a second group of letters that seemed a bit farther along.

My Dearest Natalya,   Sept 1940

The rationing has officially begun here. Fat is evidentially needed for Nitroglycerin so I guess we are now turning bacon into bombs! My how things have changed. I was glad to hear in your last letter that flights school was going well. Can just picture you in the cockpit of that PT-19. Not too sure of your group name though even you have to admit that WASP sounds more like an insect than a group of women pilots. Guess you're excited about flying here. Hopefully I will still be here at the London hospital.

The Germans have intensified their bombing here and we have been busy with the casualties. Wish you were here helping me with that bandaging technique you use to use. I should have paid more attention in that class. Evacuations have also begun so things are a bit chaotic here. Hope to hear from you soon

Love,
Emily

Katherine wished she had paid better attention in her history class. She had so many questions for her grandmother. Especially who this Emily woman was who meant so much to her grandmother. She continued to read on.

Dearest Natalya,   *January 5, 1941*

Just a brief note to let you know that I should have gone back with you when you asked me too. I'm not sure why I even hesitated. I love you and so enjoyed our time together. I never truly understood how bad it was about to become. I should have listened to you. I miss our nights huddled together in that attic room above my brothers pub. I spend most of my nights in the hospital seeing to the civilian wounded. I've seen very few soldiers. There is even talk of sending some nurses near the front lines to the field hospitals in the outskirts of Britain. I worry about you ferrying those planes and helping with anti-aircraft practice. Please be careful. I can at least take comfort in the fact that you are not here dealing with the constant shelling. Until next time.....,

Love,
Emily

Knowing how reluctant her mother and grandmother were about the past Katherine decided to do a bit of research on her own.

She quietly got up and ran downstairs to the guest bedroom where her backpack was. She stopped briefly as she peered out the window at her grandmother peacefully gardening. Katherine ran back upstairs with her tablet. She looked thru the chest for any letters that had Emily on them so she could find a last name. Finally, she came across a letter that had been stamped *'Return to Sender'*. The name on the envelope was Emily Winthrop. Suddenly the hairs on the back of Katherine's neck stood up. That was her grandmother's last name. The mystery was starting to get even more interesting. Seems like the Winthrop name was the key so that's where Katherine would start her research.

As the light drew dim Katherine realized her grandmother would be searching for her so she placed the letters carefully back in the trunk and headed towards the bedroom. She could hear footsteps coming from the stairs. Katherine quickly turned off her tablet and tossed it on her bed.

"Well dear hope you weren't too bored."

Katherine smiled as she spoke.

"So...I have a report to do for college on WWII and I'd like to ask you some questions since mom mentioned that you were stationed in London during the war."

Katherine's grandmother turned away. Katherine could see that her smile disappeared.

"Yes, dear I was there briefly. But that was such a long time ago. I'm not sure that I could help you."

Katherine knew she had to be careful about how she was going to craft the next lie.

"Yeah.... I've decided to do it on women pilots and nurses during the war.

Katherine waited for a reaction but none came. Her grandmother looked out the side window towards the garden looking suddenly melancholy.

"So Mema, is there any one memory in particular that stands out to you regarding the war?"

Katherine grabbed a pen and paper to make the lie more official.

"Eleanor Roosevelt gave a wonderful speech to women at the time. Something to the effect of no time for being patient and sitting around. We needed to fight with all our ability and that women pilots are a weapon waiting be used. My friend and classmate from nursing school kinda talked me into school."

Katherine smiled as she moved closer.

"Wow...so did you go?"

Katherine's grandmother sat down next to her as she spoke.

"Yes...I went. I flew BT-16's, UC-78's and even a JU-88 bomber. I was with the 586th IAP squadron. See the Americans and British just wanted you to move planes from manufacture to the airfields. But I wanted to see combat. I should have been careful what I asked for. Since both my parents spoke Russian in addition to Yiddish & German, I smuggled myself into Russia with the help of a woman recruiter named Lilya. You called it the USSR but Russia back then was known as the United Soviet Socialist Republic."

Katherine's grandmother got up and shook her head.

"Ahh all of those wonderful women pilots I flew with."

She grabbed a ruler that was lying on the desk and pointed at Katherine as she spoke.

"There was one pilot that flew a Yak-1. Now she was a fighter. She flew against the Germans and was shot down 3 times. I was at base when she shot down a JU-88, landed her plane and then proceeded to pass out when she got out of her plane. Incredible.... just incredible."

Katherine was scribbling down the words just as fast as her grandmother was relating them.

"Do you remember her name?"

She smiled as her grandmother answered.

"Why of course I do. It was Lilya. Not sure of her last name though. She and I had the same female mechanic, Inna I think was her name. We use to comment about her plane. It had a beautiful white rose painted on the side. Such a long time ago."

Katherine took notes on the particulars as she became immersed in her grandmother's stories.

"Ahh...but come! Dinner is ready."

CHAPTER 2

Katherine ate quietly as she watched her grandmother. Lilya was not the name on the letters she had come across upstairs.

"So…Mema…mom mentioned that you trained as a nurse?"

Her grandmother put down her fork and reached for the salad dressing.

"Yes, 2 years at the British Nursing School in London."

Katherine watched her grandmother carefully.

"And how was that?"

Her grandmother wiped the excess dressing off the rim of the carafe.

"Oh, it was good. I met the love of my life there."

Katherine was taken back by that answer and began to cough. She cleared her throat as she spoke.

"Really! So, you met grandpa in Nursing school?"

Katherine's grandmother smiled.

"Oh no child. He was the brother of Emily Winthrop, one of the women in my class. Her brother was a doctor and would take us out to lunch at the local pub. He was very handsome."

Katherine drank some tea as she thought about the letters. Her grandmother was writing to a woman not a man.

"So how was a...Emily Winthrop after you met her brother?"

"Oh, she became my best friend even during the war. Her brother was sent to train nurses in Emergency Room procedures just before the war."

Katherine watched as her grandmother got that distant look as she gazed out the dining room window. Rain was beginning to fall as Katherine's grandmother got up to bring the basket of vegetables in that she had gathered earlier. Katherine realized she might have asked too many questions but pressed on.

"So...what about your best friend? I know mine from college was supposed to come with me this trip but had to go with her dad instead."

Her grandmother sat back down as she spoke.

"Emily had a fair complexion and had beautiful long blond hair and the most intense blue green eyes I had ever seen."

Katherine noticed how her grandmother seemed to get lost in the description of Emily.

"I remember she wrote to tell me they were sending her to this Hell Hole in Corregidor."

Katherine's voice trailed as Natalya flashed back to her London apartment in the 40's. Natalya ran down the hallway to catch the phone as it rang.

"Hello? Emily! I thought I would never hear your voice again. I'm so glad you called. I...oh yes...I'm sorry. You first...."

Natalya listened intently as other women nosily hurried down the hallway.

"Yes...well...be careful. Yes...of course I'll write. Yes, I have his address."

She hung up the receiver as she realized with the nurses racing down the hallway that she was late. She picked up her purse, adjusted her skirt and ran out the door. The streets of London were awash with military convoys heading in all directions as the bus made its way to the steps of the hospital. Throughout the day she taught beginning students bandaging techniques and how to properly dress wounds. The sound of the radio and Churchill's speech was muted in the background. That day was a blur of sounds and color. When the whistle sounded for the end of the day from the factory down the road, Natalya realized she might still have time to get to the airfield to see Emily off. As Natalya took a taxi, she though she should have brought her something even though she wasn't sure if she would see her friend. She had just enough time to throw the taxi driver his fare and race to edge of the visitor's gate. She watched as other planes took off down the runway. Suddenly, there was Emily. Natalya shouted her name as she turned to face her. Emily's smile was the only thing Natalya could focus on. Emily broke thru the line and ran to Natalya.

"I didn't think I'd make it. I needed to see you off."

Emily kissed her cheek and hugged her tightly as she spoke.

"I'm so glad you did make it. So much to talk about and no time! I'll put it in a letter. Hopefully it will get to you before we reach our final destination. "

The speaker sounded the last call for Emily's flight. Each broke their embrace and waved goodbye.

Emily boarded the plane with the other nurses, placed her luggage under her seat and decided to write that letter she had promised Natalya. Periodic turbulence rocked the plane as Emily wrote. Emily placed the letter into the envelope and licked it to seal it. She knew with all the recent chaos that mail would be altered and that her letter may not arrive on time. She just needed to get the letter out and to let Natalya know how she felt. She needed to continue the connection with Natalya even thru the miles. She missed the bond they had shared during nursing school. The plane finally landed and the nurses were driven directly to a makeshift barracks while they awaited their next orders. As she stepped down from the jeep soldiers marching in the distance could be heard.

"Hello Miss Winthrop."

The young soldier smiled as he checked his satchel.

"I have your orders here. Did you arrive with the other nurses? Oh good. Then I will leave you now so I can get to the others. "

He handed her an envelope with her name on it. As she opened the letter, she smiled a nervous smile as she read her orders. By the time she arrived at her tent her battle dress, lanyard and boots were being issued to her and the other nurses. As she walked thru the encampment, she couldn't help but worry about Natalya and her love of planes. She knew that sooner or later her love of planes would get the better of her. As she rounded the corner her Commander James McNaughton called out to her.

"Winthrop! I'm sending you and 9 other nurses to Corregidor in the Philippines in a few days."

Emily breathed a sigh of relief because she had heard that being in the Philippines was safer than most places at the time.

"Yes Sir...Thank you Sir."

He raised an eyebrow as he spoke.

"Don't thank me. Evidentially the top brass thinks it's time for some tropical island R & R."

He then left and entered the tent labeled 'Office'. She headed to her tent to pack up once again.

Emily tried not to get sea sick as the plane lurched back and forth trying to avoid the turbulence. She tried to get her mind off of her current situation by remembering when she and Natalya first signed up to be military nurses. There really weren't that many decent jobs at home for women unless your "job" was to find a husband. Natalya on the other hand wanted to assert her individuality and wanted to serve. Emily remembered the time that Natalya spoke about trying to disguise herself so she could join the army because it would provide traveling and adventure that one wouldn't have to pay for. She chuckled at that idea. Emily had a hard time envisioning Natalya in the Russian military but they seemed to be willing to train women not only in flying but in military combat or so that woman recruiter said one day in the hospital lobby.

Finally, the plane landed in Manilla. A jeep took her and the 8 other nurses to a beautiful home with Bougainvillea and Plumeria in full bloom. One of the nurses even brough her golf clubs! The fragrance of the Gardenias wafted thru the air. A younger Filipino woman greeted the nurses and spoke in surprisingly good English.

"I will show you to your rooms. Freshen up and then I will show you where to eat."

Emily was shown her room. Large dark colored fans cooled the rooms. Mosquito netting was draped over the beds and as she peered thru the shades as the scent of Gardenia filtered thru.

Meals were mainly vegetables and fish. The local Filipinos did laundry and cleaning but some of us protested and did our own laundry. After several weeks of learning the routine I decided to take a break. That evening I sat down to the desk to write.

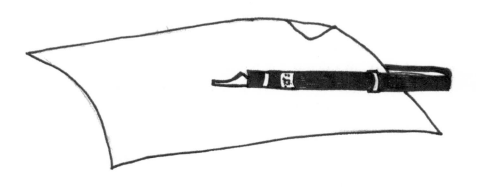

Dear Natalya,   *March 5, 1941*

We landed in Manilla this afternoon. You would love parts of this island. Sometimes it feels as though we are on a tropical island vacation. Beautifully colored orchids are everywhere. Even with the heat here the fans in our rooms make it bearable at night. We only work 4-hour day shifts. We rotate eight-hour shifts when the temperatures are cooler at night. I've mainly treated burns, blisters and the occasional upset stomach on most of the soldiers here. Needless to say, the sailors and soldiers visit quite frequently. Even here we are hearing talk of war extending. Almost wish I was back in Europe. At least I wouldn't feel so helpless. You know... as though I truly mattered. I have to admit that here we have been truly pampered. Hope your broken arm is healing nicely. Would have loved to decorate your cast! Sounds like you enjoyed the parachute training...just kidding. So ...do you finally have a favorite plane? Would love to see a picture of you in your training gear. My own private pin up girl!

Love,
Emily

The weather was windy as Emily posted the letter. It would be several weeks until she was able to write her friend again so she continued on with her day. The next month the weather was wetter and hotter as she made her way thru the mud. She balanced bandages as well as small vials of Morphine as she walked up the makeshift ramp of the tent. Gone was the tropical island country club atmosphere. Heavy equipment was being moved in from the transport ships. They were used to clear small squares of land where more tents were erected. It almost seemed like a switch was flipped as one day it was golfing on the beach to handling wave after wave of injured soldiers. It was at times surreal as she went from her tent thru the trails of jungle mud to her patients. The break that Emily was hoping for finally came as she drank the last of the coffee. She made her way back to her tent and reached for paper and pen as she sat on the cot and pulled up two crates to form a makeshift desk. She tried several pens before she found one that would finally write. Even though it was light out the tents were dimly lit. She adjusted the light of the lantern as she began to write. She wasn't sure where to start. So much activity and emotions. She wanted Natalya there so she could just hug her. She wanted to be able to have someone to confide in as the war became more surreal to her as each day passed.

Dear Natalya,   *April 1941*

We have been swamped with casualties since we moved from Manilla. The sounds of bulldozers clearing more jungle space can be heard from our tents. Some enlisted men have been helping carry blankets, sheets pillows and drugs to the newest convalescent hospital. They also have buried some of the drugs deep within the trenches. Hospital 2 went up shortly before I got here. I don't even know where here is or even what day it is! Trying to keep things dry here is an uphill battle. One of the nurses set up a small pup tent to try and keep some of the medical records dry. One of the women said at least her cleaning of pots and pans was doing her part for the war effort. She carried dirty pots that were packed dirty due to the quickness of the last move. I watched her carry them down to the stream and scrub them with sand!

Tomorrow I am to help Commander Davidson set up 7 more wards along the jungle path. Our one working radio played a message from General MacArthur that said he was sending help. One of the men set up a fence made of burlap around some rocks in the middle of the stream so we could bathe a bit more privately. The day before an enemy plane peppered the stream with bullets. Oh Natalya, it has truly been insane here. We work 20-hour days. We bathe the patients, clean wounds, change dressings and give Morphine for pain. I feel so helpless since we can't really keep things clean in the jungle.

> *We take the patients temperature but no one will see those records so why record them. I certainly don't need a thermometer to tell me whether a patient needs Quinine! High fever and chills are the norm here. How naïve I have been. What I wouldn't give for a good cup of coffee.*
>
> *Thought of you the other day and your love of Iguanas. One kept crawling under my cot. I guess he was keeping the rats away. Some of the other nurses have had their clothes shredded by those rats.*
>
> *I just want us to be together again and let the world fade out around us.*
>
> *Till Next Time,*
> *Emily*

A sudden clap of thunder brought Katherine's grandmother out of her memory and back to the present.

"Well that storm looks like it's going to be a rough one. Better get the lamps lined up."

Katherine's grandmother headed to the kitchen for the usual storm preparation. Living on the coast of Maine made for a beautiful, peaceful picturesque scene except when a storm approached from the east. Sometimes the severe wind and rain would topple old power lines or branches from the nearby woods would cross a powerline and the picture postcard cottage by the sea would become a cold and damp scene from a horror movie. So, Katherine went to the kitchen to help her grandmother place an oil lamp in every room of the house. She then added another log to the already blazing fire in the stone fireplace.

"So did your friend Emily ever survive Corregidor?"

Katherine's grandmother sat in a cozy blanket covered arm chair nearest the fireplace.

"Barely, she and several other nurses had to be rescued by one of those flying boats as I recall. Then I didn't hear from her for a long time. Never realized she was in a POW camp because of Mindanao."

Katherine watched as her grandmother curled up in the chair pulling the blanket around her. Katherine too took that opportunity to quietly head back upstairs. She took one of the smaller oil lamps with her as well as her phone. She figured even with no service she could still use the flashlight feature in addition to the lamp. She grabbed a pack of matches and headed back up to the attic room.

CHAPTER 3

❧

Katherine placed the lamp on an up righted barrel and continued to sift thru the letters in the chest. She picked up a few letters that she had not put in chronological order.

Dear Natalya,   *Feb. 23, 1941*

The German artillery landed close to us today but thank heavens we were never hit. I was using my helmet to bathe and when I heard the firing come closer, I dumped out the water and stuck the helmet on. You would have laughed if you'd seen me half naked with a helmet on my head. Needless to say, my hair was soaked and me with no curlers!

There are parts of France that are really beautiful. Wish I could tell you where we are but I'm not sure I even know the exact location. We have been moved about a lot lately in buses with blackout windows. Hope you are doing well. Hope your letter finds me this month. The logistics for this war must be a nightmare.

Miss You Terribly,
Emily

As Katherine sifted thru her grandmother's letters, she could see that these two women had a close bond. She came across a sealed letter from her grandmother to this Emily Winthrop that was stamped *'Return to Sender Unable to Deliver'*. The postmark was dated April 1942. The glue that once sealed the envelope was partially cracked and disintegrating. Katherine helped it along with the edge of her fingernail. She then carefully pulled out the letter.

Darling Emily,

    I never meant to hurt you. Lilya and I were old friends from my school days in Russia. We both dreamed of becoming pilots one day. She was in Europe trying to recruit female pilots for training. Stalin is supposedly forming all female combat units. I couldn't pass that up. So, I contacted her and as it turned out she needed a place to sleep. I offered her my bed since I was headed to the hospital. I figured I would work my shift then tell them it was my last night there. When I got there someone else was taking my shift. I looked for you but they said you were on call to the airfield. So, I made may goodbyes and went back to the apartment. You know my apartment. No couch and no furniture to speak of...not even a table. I didn't think it was a big deal to sleep next to Lilya in the bed. How was I to know you would stop by after your shift. Again, nothing happened. It seems we each have a path to follow. Unfortunately, they seem to be in different directions.

Love Always,
Natalya

Katherine soooo wished she could ask her grandmother about this letter in particular. If Emily was just a friend why was her grandmother apologizing for her sleeping with another woman. Katherine put the letter down and thought a moment. She never saw any Gay Pride flags in the house nor did she see any other indicators of her grandmother's sexual orientation. Yet it was very clear from the salutations of these letters that a bond did exist. Katherine grabbed her tablet and typed in Emily Winthrop in a search app she had loaded earlier. According to the search engine there were several Emily Winthrop's both in Washington, D.C. and in England. She narrowed the search listing Emily Winthrop's age as the same for her grandmother. Then she listed her profession during the war. Finally, she knew she had a brother.

As the search narrowed Katherine clicked on the Emily Winthrop from England. There in the photo was her Grandfather.

"Oh my gosh...Grandpa!"

She clicked again to enlarge the photo. There before her in the black and white photo stood Katherine's grandfather as a young Lieutenant with his mother, father and sister. Katherine slid the bar over and enlarged the photo of his sister...Emily Winthrop. Her name was clearly listed below the photo as was George Forester Winthrop, her grandfather. Katherine went back to the pile of letters. She tried to read the dates and put them in some type of order she found one that had a date that she couldn't read because of the dirt or possibly blood that had soaked thru the envelope. Katherine thought it might be a continuation of the last letter since on the first line was written *"You should know by now that I can't stay mad at you for long."*

> *What happened several months ago is now in the past. I just thought I would get a second chance to see you again. After working a 72-hour shift at the hospital I probably just would have slept. The female American pilots I briefly met longed for combat but would never see it since they merely shuttle planes to the airfield after they have been built. I know that's not what you wanted but it would be so much safer for you my love. We are off to the South Pacific this morning. Will continue to send my letters to that P.O. Box your brother gave me.*
>
> *Love Always, Emily*

Katherine realized that she was getting a whole different perspective on the war from reading her grandmas saved letters. She wished she knew of these letters when she had her history courses. She reached for another letter.

Dear Natalya,   March 19, 1942

It's 3 am and the jeeps loaded with casualties finally stopped. Time to catch my breath, grab a quick bite from the mess tent and see how much sleep I can get before the next wave of wounded. So many broken bodies, so many men, women and children wounded or killed. I've stopped counting. I stopped after the second day when a plane crashed into a farm house killing 3 children and maiming and burning 4 others. What were we thinking? Wanting to help and be of service sounds so trivial amidst these casualties. Last week I was in a bar listening to our soldiers bragging about how many planes they downed and how they hoped when the planes crashed over Germany that they took out more German soldiers. Have they forgotten that there are still German families with women and children in those cities? Ignore my ranting. I hope you are well and safe behind a desk somewhere far from the fighting and Blitzkrieg.

Love, Emily

Katherine straightened out another letter as she removed it from an envelope. It was sent from the Philippines.

Dearest Natalya,   April 9, 1942

Never in my various years of training had I experienced what it was like to be a combat nurse. Today was my Baptism by fire. The makeshift tents overflowed with wounded. Some stretchers were on the ground with barely recognizable men; some silent, some screaming in pain. By mid-morning I lost track of how many shots of Morphine I gave those men. We triaged them as best we could. The doctors were busy trying to reattach limbs, stop the loss of blood and try to save what was left of these poor men. We never expected to be put in charge of triage but we were in charge basically of who lived and who died. I had no time to do charts and certainly no time to process what was going on. We put signs on the foreheads of some of the badly injured soldiers listing the drugs we gave them and the dosage. Blood soaked mattresses were becoming the norm. Faces were so badly burned on some that I barely recognized them as some of the pilots I met just days before. Half the time we simply tried to make the dying men comfortable. One young man all of 16 (and yes, he lied about his age to enlist) was lying before me with both his legs gone. Another who was blinded had one of my bath towels soaked in water to try and sooth his damaged skin. Soldiers with their backsides blown away, tissue and muscles ripped off with gaping holes in their bodies was my view every day. Such carnage and horror I thought we would never get any relief. For the first time we were issued a crude form of dog tag.

We punched our name and serial number into the round metal disks. Some nurses tried to keep their sanity with humor. I'm trying to keep mine by writing you my love. You are my one connection with sanity. My one connection that lets me feel that I still have a heart and compassion. Those memories of our time together have become even more precious. I'm finally able to write this after we got a break at about 1 am. Several Army nurses and Filipino nurses arrived along with 4 other doctors. Well that's my cue!

All My Love,
Emily

Dear Natalya,   *April 28, 1942*

Sorry for the scribbling but we have been told to evacuate and that the Japanese are near. After reading your last letter dated a month ago, I do believe that the altitude at which you are flying has clouded your brain. Have you not heard that Hitler's blitzkrieg is wreaking havoc on England! Their concentration of tanks, planes and artillery along those narrow front lines have destroyed London and created not only military casualties but civilian ones as well. You and that plane of yours never get to see the real damage and death you cause. I am glad you have been ordered to visit your friend in the hospital. Maybe you will find your humanity once again by looking at the wounded, crippled and maimed bodies of your friends. I am in the thick of it here and hope I have not lost you forever. We are awaiting transport off this godforsaken island. My friend Alice said she would post this letter to you when she gets to the mainland.

Love,
Emily

Katherine noticed as she reached for another letter that there seemed to be a gap in the dates. The next letter from Emily isn't until March 1945. She looked thru the rest of the envelopes and down in the chest. There are a few letters to Emily but since Katherine was trying to keep her timeline correct those letters didn't enter the time line until the end of the war. Katherine heard the footsteps coming up the stairs. Katherine quickly threw the letters back in the chest and grabbed her oil lamp, tablet and shot downstairs to her room.

"My goodness! Sounds like a heard of elephants up here. What were you doing?"

Katherine smiled and opened her tablet.

"Oh, just exploring. I was coming down to you and then I remembered I forgot to turn my tablet off so.... I ran back up here to shut it off."

Katherine figured that would have worked for her mother. She just hoped now it worked for her grandmother.

"Well I wanted to let you know that the cable is out but I have some video tapes that I rented last week if you want to watch a movie with me?"

Katherine closed her tablet and stood up.

"Sounds good! Let's go! Oh...do you have popcorn?"

Katherine's grandmother smiled.

"Well of course I have popcorn. How else would I enjoy a movie?"

CHAPTER 4

As Katherine sorted thru her grandmother's videos, she noticed that the majority of them were war movies: *1917, A Hidden Life, Midway, JoJo Rabbit,* and *The Battle of Jangsari.* But then she noticed 2 that were hidden towards the back of the cabinet. *Desert Hearts* & *Claire of the Moon* were both films dealing with Lesbian relationships. Katherine decided to perform her own test.

"Hey Memaw how about this movie Desert Hearts?"

Her grandmother paused as she turned to face Katherine.

"Oh no dear. I don't think that's a movie you will like."

"But why? I've heard the music in it is quite good."

Her grandmother placed the other videos back into the cabinet.

"Well if that's what you want to watch...go ahead and load it into the machine."

As the two women watched the movie the lightning and thunder passed over the house and into the distance. Rain in various intensities fell on the roof echoing throughout the well-built cottage. Another log was added to the fireplace as Katherine noticed moisture that reflected off of her grandmother's cheek. She looked back at the screen as the two main characters kissed as the rain came down. It was then that Katherine felt an emptiness in the pit of her stomach. Her grandmother had fallen in love with this Emily Winthrop during the war. But why wasn't she with her now Katherine wondered. Grandpa died over 25 years ago. Katherine realized she wasn't going to get answers unless she spoke with her grandmother. She picked up the controller, reached up and paused the movie.

"Memaw...can I ask you a question?"

"Of course, child."

Katherine turned to face her grandmother.

"Did you truly love Emily Winthrop?"

Katherine's grandmother turned and stood up obviously agitated.

"How on earth...where did you..."

She looked up towards the attic. Her face changed to a scowl as she headed up the stairs towards the attic. Katherine knew she was in trouble but couldn't keep up the ruse any longer.

"Memaw wait!"

Katherine ran after her as she navigated the living room furniture to try and get to her grandmother. But she was quick and fueled by anger and determination as she reached the landing of the stairs. She stopped briefly at the door to the attic then went in. Katherine missed her by 4 steps as she entered the attic slightly behind her grandmother.

"Memaw...please let me explain. I was bored and I thought it would be cool to explore this part of the house since I had never been up here. I do have a report but it's not due till the end of Spring. I'm sorry"

Her grandmother already had the chest open and held one of the groups of envelopes.

"These were personal! You should have never touched them let alone read them! They are my memories not yours!"

As she yelled at Katherine, tears welled up in her grandmother's eyes. She placed the envelopes up to her nose and breathed in the faint scent of Lavender. She remembered the time when Emily was angry at her for describing her peaceful feeling flying planes of war while people below were dying. She looked down at the chest and reached for a letter that was already unbundled.

My Dear Natalya,   *March 1945*

    As I stare out the window of my hospital room, I realized that I needed to try and connect with you once more. So much time has passed I'm not even sure if I can write all the things that have happened.

    After we were evacuated from Corregidor, we were flown to Mindanao so our planes could refuel. But Murphy's Law struck and our plane was the one that got damaged after takeoff. The other plane we heard later made it safely to Australia. Ten of us scrounged whatever we could and patiently waited for transport but it never came. We had to surrender to the Japanese on May 10ᵗʰ 1942. That's the last date I truly remember with any certainty. I think it was Sept 9ᵗʰ that I arrived with the other nurses and soldiers at Santo Tomas Internment Camp. Civilians ran the camp for a while and life was manageable. Days turned into weeks and weeks into months.

    As the food ran out and we had no energy to move around people started getting sick. One of the nurses got Scurvy. Peoples clothing and shoes were wearing thin. We were even using sheets for underwear and tying pieces of wood to our feet with hemp for shoes. We used bamboo knitting needles that one of the soldiers made. We knitted socks, bras and panties.

My mother, G-d rest her soul, would have been proud. Once the Japanese military relieved the civilian's things got worse. The Red Cross packages would be opened by their soldiers and punctured with their bayonets. Then they would leave the packages in the sun to spoil with the canned meat and other food. They also cut off supplies of medicine, blood plasma and equipment needed for surgery. We had no tools nor seeds to plant although bananas were harvested from around the camp. Yet, we managed to survive. The camp was truly hell! Teeth pulled with no anesthesia and even the entertainment although not great was stopped. I looked in the mirror the other day and I looked like one of those Halloween skeletons...really! My body is hideous. Nothing but skin and bones. But what do you expect being given 6 ounces of food a day? Banana trees were cut down, cats were gone and one of the soldiers dared another to cook a rat he had caught. I cried when I saw those American troops bursting thru the camp gates. I dropped to my knees and continued to sob like a baby. The nurses said they would remember that date as long as they lived.

Once I found out what the date was, I realized how truly long we had been in that prison. The date was February 3, 1945. Several of the nurses even said they were getting a tattoo with the name of the soldier that first helped them into the trucks that drove us out of the camp.

I am writing to you from the 12th General Hospital on Leyte Island. In another two weeks I should be in San Francisco. Guess that is around the 24th of February. I will try to post this with my brother in hopes that it will get to you. All I can do is pray that you are back on European soil and keeping your feet on the ground.

Love,
Emily

"I received this letter after 4 years of not hearing from her. At first, I thought she was dead. My brain couldn't accept that thought. I kept writing to her even though I couldn't locate her or her brother. I never dreamed all that time she was a POW.

I remember flying troops into Poland. We liberated a prison camp in Auschwitz when we ran into the British along the same road. I remember him handing me the envelope and my stuffing it into my jacket pocket as the soldiers were getting sick and throwing up over what they were seeing. I had just finished writing this one to Emily."

The post mark was January 1945 as Katherine's grandmother ripped open the letter briefly glanced at the beginning and handed it to Katherine.

Dearest Emily,   *Jan 1949*

For years I have been writing you letters refusing to believe that you are dead. What other explanation could there be? You should have returned from the South Pacific a while ago with the other nurses yet no one seems to know where you are.

This morning's sight as we flew in troops to Poland was more than anyone could bare. Our Soviet troops liberated this POW camp in Auschwitz. I have never in my life seen a walking skeleton. We were told they were gassing men, women and children but didn't believe it until we came across their bodies. First a pile of shoes, then a pile of clothes piled 2 stories high. And then we came upon the trenches with bodies piled 4 feet high. How can one human being do that to another human being Emily?

I am worried that the safety I thought you had no longer exists. I am making plans to stay in Europe and will try to get your brother to help me.

Love Always,
Natalya

Katherine read the letter realizing that her grandmother seemed to be reliving those emotions over again.

"What did you do after you read her letter?"

Katherine's grandmother looked around and sat down.

"I tried to find her brother but it was absolute chaos with all the allies liberating towns and celebrating. The German soldiers that surrendered were transported to various humane prisons. I switched uniforms with an American soldier who was collecting souvenirs. I then made my way towards France and from there I went to London. About a month later I finally found him only to find out that Emily had died while in that island hospital. He was very nice to me and for several months we dated. He then asked for my hand in marriage. You obviously know what happened next. But I never forgot my Emily."

Natalya was hunched over the chest of letters as wave after wave of tears hit her body. Katherine got up and went to her grandmother hugging her and sobbing along with her.

"I am so sorry Memaw. I never wanted to hurt you. I was stupid to even think that this was just some simple story. I..."

Suddenly Katherine looked up. It was if a lightbulb went off in her head.

"Wait a minute...You said her brother told you Emily had died in that hospital on Leyte Island in 1945, right?"

Katherine's grandmother looked up at Katherine trying to dry her eyes on her shirtsleeve.

"Yes, he did. Even when we were married, he disliked that I went to church each weekend in February to mourn her."

Katherine placed the letter she had read back in the chest.

"Wait here!"

Katherine ran down the steps to her room and searched for her tablet. She threw her normally neat clothes in the air as she searched for her tablet. Finally, she knelt down and looked under her bed. There to the side underneath her sweater was the tablet. She prayed she had remembered to charge it. As she turned it on her mind was trying to place all the facts that her grandmother had told her together with what she remembered that last time she had done the research. There in her tablet's memory was what she was looking for. She quickly ran back upstairs with tablet in hand.

"Look Memaw...see..."

Katherine folded the tablet back and held the screen in front of her.

"Emily Winthrop didn't die on that date. As a matter of fact, according to this she is still alive and living in England!"

CHAPTER 5

Natalya awoke to a headache she hadn't felt since her flying days. Just as she thought last evenings conversation was a dream, she saw a note on her nightstand. There, in her granddaughters handwriting was Emily's name with an address and phone number. As she dressed, she thought about the war. She thought about how after inquiring about Emily and hearing that she died, her love of planes and being in the air suddenly seemed to die with her. She stopped at Katherine's room to find her granddaughter still asleep. She headed up the stairs to the attic.

The attic door creaked open as the morning sun began to filter thru the window. She sat down next to the chest and filtered thru the letters Katherine had already opened and left on the top of the blankets. She then found the letter she was looking for. The letter that she had sent Emily when she finally flew the Soviet planes in the war. The letter that caused Emily to be angry with her. The letter that, as she read it over again, realized how arrogant and naive it sounded.

Dear Emily,   March 1942

I know that life is never how you plan it to be. Several of us had the opportunity to make what we thought was a difference so we took it. I wish I could describe to you the calm, quiet peacefulness I feel when I'm in the air. It is only the noise of the machine guns when we are attacking those German Luftwaffe planes that breaks the silence amongst the clouds. We clear the way while the bombers hang back and line up their targets. Yes, it's dangerous but the adrenaline rush is incredible.

I remember when we said we wanted to be of service and how we thought being on the ground was the safe place to be. Now I know that the place to be is up here among the clouds and not with those bleeding and broken bodies you want to take care of. I admire you for sticking to your convictions and nursing those soldiers. At least I can rest assured that you are far away from the front lines and safe from the shelling. I'm not sure when this letter will find you but I want you to know that I miss you and hope we will cross each other's path soon.

Love Always,
Natalya

"How could I have been so stupid. Such and ass!"

Natalya chastised herself as she sifted thru more letters.

Dearest Emily,   March 1942

Your last letter made me sad to know that you were in such a horrid place both physically and mentally. I would surely gone mad feeling like a caged dog waiting for his turn to be shot.

I have gone from the silence of my cockpit to the sound of crunching ampules under my feet and clanking thermometers. We have been ordered to visit some of our wounded comrades at the hospital in Sochi. Loud bells rang in a distant ward when a patient would take a turn for the worst. The strong smells of Ether and Chloroform created such a sicken sweet smell that it made my stomach turn. As I walked the halls searching for my friends, I would get a whiff of Sauerkraut and tobacco. Then it was back to alcohol, medications and wilted flowers from the bedsides. I would definitely have preferred the smell of my leather bomber jacket and the transmission fluid of my cockpit. I am sorry you are experiencing such horror where you are.

I wish I could show you the silence and beauty of the clouds. Other than in your arms it is the only other place I have found peace. We have been told that the Germans are on the run. What I do know is that I can't wait to get back up in the air. You need to get yourself away from that island in the Pacific and back to the safety of England my love. After hearing the news of Pearl Harbor, I fear for your safety on Corregidor.

You are always in my heart,
Natalya

"Such arrogance!"

Natalya threw the letters across the floor. She looked up as one of the letters landed next to a pink fuzzy slipper.

"Memaw? "

Katherine yawned as she tried to stop squinting at the now sunlit room.

"What's wrong?"

Katherine came further into the room and sat on a box full of cushions and bedspreads.

"I was such an arrogant fool. I hadn't read those letters since the war. Years after my marriage to Emily's brother who was your grandfather, he gave them to me as a peace offering one night after one of our arguments. I put them in that trunk and never looked at them until now."

Katherine could see that her grandmother had tears in her eyes. She felt around the pocket of her robe and found a tissue. She knelt down next to her grandmother and handed her the tissue.

"Maybe you should try talking to her. I mean...after all these years to find each other again I would think would be a good thing."

Natalya reached over and kissed her granddaughter on the forehead

"Perhaps you're right. Since there is such a time difference, I think I will write her."

Katherine got up yawned and stretched.

"I'm going to get dressed. How about I make breakfast for a change."

Natalya stood up and picked up the strewn letters and placed them back in the chest.

"That sounds good. I have to hunt for some paper anyway."

Katherine looked back at her grandmother.

"Well I know it's not very romantic but I have some college ruled paper in my backpack."

Both women headed down the stairs…Katherine returned to her room to dress and Natalya to check her desk in the study for pen and paper.

As Katherine's grandmother sat at the table, she watched her granddaughter cooking.

"Katherine dear… can I ask you something?"

Katherine grabbed the toast from the toaster and scrambled the eggs as she answered.

"Of course, Memaw…anything."

Natalya turned her chair slightly to face Katherine.

"How did you feel when you found out I was gay?"

Katherine turned and gasped at her grandmother.

"Oh, my G-d ! You're Lesbian?"

Katherine smiled when she realized that her grandmother took her gasp seriously.

"Obviously I'm joking Memaw. I think it's cool. My roommate in college is gay. She says she is bisexual but it's been 3 years and I've only seen her go out with women. Does momma know?"

Natalya got up and went to get some juice.

"I've never mentioned it to her so if you don't mind, for now can we keep this our little secret?"

Katherine laughed as she sat the plates of food on the table.

"Gee …let me think. A college kid keeping a secret from her mom…hammam. Yeah, I think I can pull it off!"

Natalya placed the juice glasses down.

"I never knew I raised you to be such a smart ass!"

After breakfast Katherine and her grandmother took a walk down the road from the cottage that led to the rocky coastline that was Maine. Katherine talked about her college courses, her mother's boyfriends and her various friends at college. Natalya relaxed as she watched her very animated granddaughter navigate over the rocks as she moved the seaweed to view the shoreline creatures. She realized how time had passed and how much different her granddaughter was from her at that age. It seemed to Natalya that today's generation dealt with injustice immediately and didn't let much grass grow under their feet. On their way back Natalya proved her point by asking Katherine a question.

"Katherine dear, how would you have handled the realization that someone you loved and was told were dead was now alive?"

Without missing a beat Katherine answered.

"Well, since I once loved them, I would definitely make contact with them or at least try to. Cause you never know what things they may have been told about me. At least that's what I would do."

Natalya smiled at her granddaughter as they entered the cottage.

"How about I make us some hot chocolate?"

Katherine smiled as she sat down by the fire with her textbooks.

"Oooh…that sounds great Memaw. And how about some of those scones you made yesterday?"

Natalya patted her granddaughter on the head as she headed into the kitchen.

As she heated the milk and prepared the chocolate, she realized her granddaughter was right. The two women had shared a loving relationship no matter how brief it was. They always tried to communicate with each other during difficult periods of wartime. Natalya made her decision as she poured the thickened hot chocolate into her favorite teapot. Once the scones were taken from the tin on the shelf and arranged onto the plate with Katherine's favorite cat mugs Natalya picked up the tray and headed into the living room. Katherine seemed quite comfortable laying on the floor in front of the fireplace ensconced in one of her textbooks. Natalya laid the tray beside her, poured herself a mug of hot chocolate and headed over to the desk. She checked the drawers for paper and finally chose a light pastel paper. She smiled as she looked over at her granddaughter remembering her offer of her college ruled notebook paper. She grabbed her fountain pen, took a sip from her mug and began to write.

Dear Emily,   *January 2ⁿᵈ, 2019*

I am not sure I know where to begin. Your brother George proposed to me shortly after the war. I tried writing you and it wasn't until I tried to go thru the war office that he then informed me that you were dead. I was naturally devastated. Afterall, the war had ended and everyone was celebrating yet I was in mourning. George even gave me some letters that had 'Return TO Sender' on them.

I kept all our letters in a trunk until my granddaughter came across them. She was doing a report for college and was asking me a lot of questions about the war. I never forgot about you and those questions she was asking just brought up old wounds and memories. When she looked up your name on her computer, she found that you were alive and living at this address!

Age has taken its toll on my body but I would love to come and visit you. Since the time frame is a bit of an issue My granddaughter Katherine has set up an email account for me so that perhaps correspondence would be a bit easier. The email is ladyhawke5849@yahoo.com I would love to talk with you again please....

Love Always,
Natalya

Natalya carefully folded the letter and placed it carefully into the envelope. She looked over as she saw Katherine curled up with a pillow and blanket sprawled amongst her books. Natalya quietly got up and placed the letter in the mailbox for afternoon pickup.

Days passed as Natalya and Katherine talked more about the war and they brought the letters down in hopes of better organizing them. Days turned into weeks as Natalya religiously checked the mailbox. Katherine watched as her grandmother would quicken her pace to the mailbox only to be rejected by an empty box of advertisements and coupons. Katherine hesitated checking the email she had set up for her grandmother. She realized that maybe Emily Chase Winthrop was more adapted to technology then her beloved Memaw and that she would use this system once she got her Memaw's letter.

"Memaw? Why don't you check your email today? Afterall it is possible that she may use that instead of snail mail or regular mail."

She made a face and grunted as she came in from checking the mailbox. She headed towards the desk in the living room and sat down as she starred at the laptop.

"Do you need some help signing in?"

Katherine pulled a chair over from the dining table in anticipation of a "yes" answer. She knew her grandmother wasn't too comfortable with the computer since there were many times, she would try to email her and would get no response until after she would call her grandmother and guilt her into using it.

"Oh, I suppose so. You know how I hate this thing."

Katherine knew that once her grandmother got use to using the laptop it would become a love hate relationship. Katherine laughed as she opened up the laptop.

"I never meant to pull you kicking and screaming into the modern age Memaw. I just thought it was easier and faster to show you pictures and let you in on the family gossip."

Katherine would always send her grandmother photos of her travels and adventures in college. Her grandmother would then stick them on her refrigerator and framed the ones she really liked. Katherine thought it would be easier to pick and choose from the photos she was now sending her now that she had a new camera phone. She remembers talking her mother into getting grandma Natalya a laptop & printer for Christmas. Katherine spent weekends coming up from college to play computer teacher to her Memaw. But true to form…. when Katherine left so did her grandmothers' interaction with the laptop. Never did Katherine dream how much that was about to change.

As she went step by step with her instructions, she watched her grandmother gingerly tap the keys of the laptop. Finally, she reached the Yahoo site. Katherine reached over and took the mouse from her grandmother.

"Here...I'm going to put this Yahoo icon on your Desktop so all you have to do is click on it."

As Katherine clicked on the icon her grandmother reached for her hand suddenly.

"Oh, my G-d!"

Katherine looked up at the screen.

"She wrote back!"

The two women starred momentarily at the screen, one in disbelief and the other in welcomed relief. Katherine handed the mouse back to her grandmother.

"Here Memaw, Its okay.... I'll be over here on the sofa."

Natalya quickly grabbed her hand and squeezed it.

"No ...stay...please...it's okay."

It was as if Katherine suddenly became a sense of security for Natalya.

"Okay...I'm here."

As Katherine read the letter, she hoped that this Emily person that she got to know thru the letters remembered her grandmother. She never realized until now that her grandmother might get hurt depending upon what this email said. She wanted to give her grandmother privacy yet at the same time was extremely curious. Katherine quickly read the email then glanced over at her grandmother. She watched as her Memaw seemed to read every word as tears ran down her cheek. Katherine handed her a tissue, kissed her on the cheek and went over to sit down on the couch.

My Dearest Natalya,   **January 21, 2019**

I nearly cried when I received your letter. My brother told me you had died after your plane crashed somewhere over Berlin on May 9th , 1945. Of the many things I will never forget….that date is one of them. I was rescued along with 65 other Army nurses and spent days after arriving in California searching for you and trying to reach my brother. It was an insane time. Happy that the war was finally over, people trying to find loved ones not knowing if they were in hospitals, liberated concentration camps or dead. I finally returned to my family here in Harrogate.

I pretty much keep to myself since my dad passed shortly after the war. Mom died about 8 years ago giving up her share in one of the many spas in the area. Now the area caters to the wealthy who spend thousands of pounds to bathe in iron, Sulphur and salt.

So, did you ever marry? Am I to assume that you turned my brother down after he proposed? The letter carries your maiden name yet you mentioned that you have a granddaughter so….I guess you will explain with your next email.

It's been almost 75 years so I'm sure time is something we both have had to adjust to. After my accident on Santo Tomas time has not been kind to my body either. Would love to hear more about your daughter, granddaughter and you.

Love,
Emily

Katherine looked up from her book as her grandmother bowed her head.

"What's wrong Memaw?"

Natalya looked up at the screen of the laptop.

"Well? How did it go? I admit I couldn't resist so I read the first part. It seemed positive."

Katherine placed her textbook down, got up and walked to her Memaw. She placed a hand on her shoulder as she spoke.

"So? Was it a favorable letter?"

"Oh, sweetheart it was a wonderful letter. She wants us to write to one another for a while."

Katherine could tell that there was something else her grandmother was thinking about.

"So, what's wrong?"

Natalya pushed back against the desk as the chair legs drug the floor. As she rung her hands, she looked out the window.

"I suppose I just can't fathom how two people who were so intimate can now seem so far apart."

Katherine knelt down to face her grandmother.

"Well then, I guess you'll just have to fill in that gap.

Natalya turned around, sighed and began to type a reply to her beloved Emily.

Dear Emily,   **January 22, 2019**

I am glad to have connected with you again. I'm sorry to say that it seems as though your brother controlled us both. After he proposed and told me you were dead, I didn't really know what to do. I was lost and alone. There were so many things I had to say to you and now it was too late. I married your brother shortly after his proposal. We settled in Florida for a while and after I had our daughter Lianna Winthrop things seemed fine for a while. The war changed a lot of people and your brother was one of them. George became abusive. Since I never knew where you were buried, I would go to this tiny cemetery in our area and I would sit there and pay my respects. Your brother George hated that and by the time I came home he was drunk and violent. He eventually got help but then he started seeing another woman that was half my age. It took me 10 years but I was finally able to take Lianna and leave him.

Enough about George please tell me what happened to you in the Philippines? Why were there no records of you or what happened? You mentioned accident .... what happened?

Till next time...Love You,
Natalya

Katherine yawned as she closed her textbook. The little animated clock chimed 7 pm as she looked out the window at the night sky approaching.

"How about I make dinner tonight Memaw?"

Katherine watched as her grandmother starred at the laptop screen after pressing 'send'. She figured keeping her busy was just as important as her learning about email. She walked over to her grandmother, took the mouse and showed her how to look up things on the internet.

"See, it is literally that easy to look up events or people. Just be careful on certain sites cause sometimes they charge you for looking up the information. But these are the sites you kinda wanna stick to."

Katherine watched as her grandmother slowly moved the mouse and started typing in certain places from the war. Since she was well occupied Katherine headed to the kitchen to make the Spaghetti dinner.

CHAPTER 6

Storm clouds gathered in the west as Emily looked out her window. The flickering of lightening could be seen in the distance. The rain pelted the window as Emily read Natalya's email. She reached for her wool sweater, made a cup of tea and sat down at the desk. As she read Natalya's words, she remembered her brother being a jerk to her on several occasions during the war. He was the one who said he would try and help navigate the sending of the letters from Natalya to his sister yet there were times he seemed that he couldn't be bothered. She remembered shortly after she was rescued from the internment camp and arrived at the 126th General Hospital on Leyte Island how she managed to pull some strings to get a call into her brother.

"Oh George, its soo good to hear a familiar voice. Sorry.... I don't mean to sob in your ear. Have you heard from Natalya? What do you mean you haven't heard anything in several months? Was she captured? What was her last letter I mean where was it from? Why are you being like this? Of course, I care about you and think of you. Of course, I can't wait to see you. George? Hello? George?"

Emily remembered that conversation well since had she not been upset after it, she would have seen the fuel truck collide with one of the jeeps as she walked across the compound. The blast set her clothes on fire and punctured her eardrum on that left side. She thought the hospital was being bombed. She felt someone padding the flames out as another person helped her up. Second degree burns on the left side of her face also left her unable to hear well on that side. Emily put her wool sweater on as she started typing on the computer.

My Darling Natalya, January 23, 2019

You are so right. My brother was an ass. I just never knew how much. The day of my accident I had managed to get a call out to him. When I asked him how you were, he went into this tirade and acted like some jealous schoolboy! He actually hung up on me when I asked why he was being so difficult. When I left the communications tent and headed back across the compound, I never saw the fuel tanker hit a jeep until it was too late. Due to where I was and the distance from it, I received 2nd degree burns on the left side of my face and body. Guess the sexy senior swimsuit edition is out of the question?

Anyway, I had to wait till California to get skin grafts and as long as you talk to my right side …. I might actually hear you so we are good! Do you have pictures of your daughter and granddaughter? Sounds like your granddaughter likes spending time with you. How is your daughter doing? How are you doing? Other than those two is there anyone else special in your life?

Love, Emily

She turned to see her reflection in the widow as the rain eased up. She turned slightly and brushed her hair away from her left side exposing that side of her scarred face. Emily's hands felt slightly down her left shoulder. The scars although well healed on the outside never really healed on the inside. She looked at the circles under her eyes as the night terrors of that fateful day never went away. Emily walked to her hallway closet and pulled out a step stool as she reached for a box carefully hidden on the back shelf. It was kept closed by an old pink ribbon tied neatly around the top and bottom of the box. She closed the closet door and sat down on the cushion that sat on top of the window box.

As she untied the ribbon she wondered if she was doing the right thing by reconnecting with Natalya. When she opened the box there on top sat a worn 3x5 photograph of her and Natalya. Of all the photographs of her family, acquaintances and places she had traveled it was rather odd that this is the photograph that was on top. She remembered the day that photograph was taken. She spent the night with Natalya and had to rush to get into their uniforms thinking they were both on call and realized halfway there that they were off. Natalya forced her to pull over in a field and positioned the camera on a tree stump to then take their picture in front of their jeep. War was imminent yet she remembered never wanting to leave that bed or that room. As she smiled those memories came back as clear as day. She remembered the white roses Natalya brought her along with the rare chocolate candy bar. They went to dinner around the corner at a little well- known Bistro. Emily watched Natalya's lips as she spoke about the day's events and how she didn't think that Germany would start the war. They had known each other for a while and had been flirting off and on quietly at work but nothing ever continued except for today when Natalya asked her to an evening out. She remembered trying on three very plain dresses realizing those were the only clothes she had other than her uniforms. Even her hair was not cooperating as she removed the pin curls underneath her scarf. She remembered Natalya's smile as she handed her the roses and chocolates at the little secluded table in the back of the Bistro. Emily chuckled slightly as she remembered the wine but couldn't remember what they ate. But her brain was suddenly remembering everything else about that evening. Once at the door to Emily's room at the top of the stairs Natalya kissed her gently on the cheek as she thanked her for a wonderful evening. As Natalya turned to walk back down the stairs Emily didn't want her to go.

"Hey...why don't you come in for a bit and enjoy that chocolate with me?"

Natalya turned and smiled as she quickly hopped up the steps and into Emily's room. The two women embraced as Natalya kissed Emily on the lips. This time passion gave way to politeness. Natalya placed her hands softly against Emily's breast as her nipples responded. Emily placed passionate kisses down Natalya's neck and shoulder. Slowly buttons became undone and Emily remembers how her shirt slid off her shoulders and onto the floor. Natalya cupped her bra in her hand as her fingers moved up Emily's bra straps and around to the back hooks. Emily's pulse quickened as Natalya's lips caressed her now very erect nipple. Both women had backed up to the wall beside Emily's bed. Emily wanted to touch Natalya and feel the softness of her skin as her emotions became confused and excited all at the same time. She unbuttoned Natalya's shirt to find not a bra but a very silky camisole that added to sensuousness against her fingers. She pulled it up from her skirt to reveal Natalya's beautifully tanned, well- toned body.

"You are so exquisite. You take my breath away."

Emily kissed Natalya's lips for what seemed like the first time. As she leaned in to her she could feel Natalya's hardened nipples against her own. Natalya backed her up onto the bed as she knelt on top of her. She kissed her belly as she moved down to her skirt line. The warmth Emily felt between her legs was building with each of Natalya's kisses. She unbuttoned the side button and slid both the skirt and the cream- colored slip off and down Emily's now quivering legs. Natalya unclipped each panty hose leg as she rolled them off of Emily's legs. She sat up in response, not sure of what she was feeling. Natalya whispered in her ear.

"Shuuu…it's okay. I want to taste you. I promise …. I won't hurt you."

Emily laid back as Natalya gently spread her legs. Emily could feel her lips against her mound as fingers gently separated the lips.

Natalya's firm, moist tongue flicked against Emily's clit. Once, twice, three times she moved wanting to continue that feeling. Finally, Natalya plunged her tongue deep into Emily's sex. Never before had she experienced a feeling such as this.

"Oh...please don't...don't stop. I've never felt this way."

As Natalya's tongue worked Emily's sex, her fingers reached up and rolled Emily's nipples between her fingers. Her heart pounded as it felt it would come out of her chest. She grabbed the bedsheet with one hand and held Natalya tightly to her as she came in explosive waves of pleasure. A clap of thunder and lightning suddenly raised Emily from her memory. She sighed heavily as she realized that the flashback would cause her to now change her panties. She placed the photo back in the box and stood up as the howling wind, thunder and lightning hit. The sensual memory had put her in a relaxed state yet now her body was reacting to something totally different.

Emily hated the loud sounding storms. Severe storms brought back her fight-or-flight response from the war. In her apartment, the walls were not thick enough to keep the sounds of weather and war out. Her heart pounded faster, her blood pressure was rising and her muscles were tightening. But unlike normal response where the body is ready to react for safety and then calms down, her nervous system couldn't return to its normal state of balance. There were times when Emily couldn't move. She reached for her little portable DVD she had on the table, took her headphones and ran into the closet in the hallway. She placed her headphones on, turned on the little DVD player and watched her favorite calm down movie…. *'Ladyhawke'.*

CHAPTER 7

❧

"Well my dear that was very good spaghetti. The sauce had enough garlic to keep the vampires away for a week!"

Natalya chuckled as she ate the last meatball in her bowl.

"You know I'm just teasing, don't you?"

Katherine got up and collected her grandmothers' plate as she stuck her tongue out at her. As the two women laughed, a familiar ding sound came from the laptop. It was the windows version of 'You've Got Mail'. Katherine's grandmother practically flew out of the dining room chair and headed for the desk. Katherine smiled as she headed in the kitchen to finish the dishes.

There on the laptop was a flashing curser indicating that Emily had responded. It had to be her since Natalya never used the email for anything other than her conversation with Emily. As she moved the mouse and read the email her eyes focused on the sentence that described Emily's accident. She read the sentence over and over again. Emily had survived so much already and now disfigurement. Natalya's granddaughter had showed her how to scan and send photos since that was what the laptop was originally for. She wanted to reach thru the screen and hold Emily. She rummaged through the drawers of the desk to find the photo a neighbor had taken of the three women last year. It was Katherine's favorite even though her mom hated it because she said it made her look old like her grandmother. Once she found it, she scanned it and placed it into the file Katherine made for her simply entitled 'Emily'. Natalya then sat back and began to type.

Dearest Emily,   **January 24, 2019**

I had no idea of your accident. So many things I wish I could change. But I truly didn't know. I sent you a photo that one of our neighbors took when my daughter and granddaughter were with me last year. There have been a few mild interests over the years but nothing special. I finally resolved that living alone seemed a better option. The occasional visits from my granddaughter Katherine makes it enjoyable. My daughter still blames me for the rough relationship I had with her father. Some things she doesn't need to know such as his girlfriends in town and his excessive drinking when he wanted to lay in bed with me. It was as if he needed that extra liquid courage to practically rape me during sex. I'm sorry, I didn't mean to talk about that but I guess it shows how he changed since the war. I suppose I agreed to marry him because he was my only connection to you. You were soft and gentle while he was hard and rough. You were always so optimistic and kind while he was negative and rude. He even kicked a puppy I got when my daughter Lianna was born. It was barking and wanted to play but he was frustrated that I was paying more attention to Lianna. And the puppy. What was really hard was when Katherine was born and she resembled you. When she was growing up, she so wanted her grandfather to do things with her. But he refused, would insult her and yell at her when she would cry at the things he said.

Oh Emily, I so want her to meet you. I want her to see the woman who always held my heart. I know we are both older but that should be one more reason why we should see each other again. Time is not our friend. I could come visit you. Or better yet, you could come here to Lubec, Maine. It is a quiet place right by the coast. The nearest neighbor is a couple miles away and the town is a quiet seaside type village.

No hustle and bustle unless you prefer that sort of thing. In which case I could come to you!

Please consider my request. How about your life? Guess I should have asked if you were with someone. Not very familiar with Harrogate, England.

Love,
Natalya

Natalya thought for a moment about what she had written about Emily's brother George. But then she realized she was angry at the secrets that had been kept and the damage that George had caused. She pressed 'send'. Katherine brought two bowls of cherry Jell-O and sat one down on the desk in front of her grandmother.

"So? How's it going? What did Emily say?"

Katherine took a heaping spoon of Jell-O and didn't bother to chew. She swallowed as she waited for a response from her grandmother.

"Well, it's a bit difficult to stay in control but I'm working on it. At least we are talking. So many things that weren't said due to the war. So many things lied about for the good of the families. I sent her that photograph I like so much of you, your mom and I."

As Katherine sat on the edge of the sofa, she was excited to hear more.

"So, is she going to send a picture of herself to you? You know...so you can see what each other looks like?"

Natalya's smile went away. She bowed her head as she looked at the laptop screen.

"I don't think so since she had an accident during the war. It left her face and left side scarred. So, I don't think she will be sending a photo of herself."

Katherine's smile faded as she empathized with her grandmother.

"Sorry Memaw I think you were kind of expecting that."

Natalya turned and touched her granddaughters' knee.

"Hey, it's okay. This is a good thing here. We are reconnecting. Her personality still shines thru in her letters. And that happened because of you!"

Natalya finished her Jell-O and stood up. She pulled up her sweater from the back of the chair, put it on and rolled the sleeves up.

"I need some air dear. Mind if I take a walk? I just need to clear my head."

Katherine knew what that meant. Her Memaw wanted to be alone. Katherine gathered her books and headed upstairs.

"I'm going to take my shower while you're out. Don't worry…I promise not to use all the hot water."

As Natalya opened up the front door the cool wind gave no indication that summer was even in the area. She zipped up her all- weather jacket and shut the door behind her. She took in a deep breath as she decided to walk along the coast line for a change instead of her normal woods walk. She tried desperately to get a handle on her emotions as the smell of the salt air filled her nostrils. Why didn't she push for poof of Emily's death? She loved flying planes and loved the adrenalin rush that engaging in combat caused. But her love for Emily was new and just beginning to grow. She could have come back to Europe sooner.

She could have postponed the celebrations and headed back to Emily. After seeing the prison camps in Germany first hand after landing the Russian troops, she couldn't possibly imagine what it was like for her gentle Emily to be in one of those camps on the Philippine islands such as Bataan or Corregidor. And then there was the accident that left Emily disfigured. She always thought that she could have passed for a man and sometimes did in order to get to fly P0-2's until she learned of Russia's enlisting of women combat pilots. Emily was always the porcelain- skinned beauty that would turn heads when they entered the USO or the pubs. As she climbed over a rather large rock that overlooked the small harbor, she knew there really wasn't anything she could do at this stage about the past. She could only made amends and change what was clearly in her present path. No matter what Emily looked like her personality was still there. Natalya figured that was better than most of the women she met years after the war. She smiled briefly as she remembered portions of time with various women, some for companionship and some simply for sex. None seemed to have the right balance of the qualities she found with Emily.

"Why am I even debating this? You've been tending to that garden of yours for way too long Natalya. You need to make contact with that part of the world that has Emily in it!"

As if giving herself a pep talk out loud Natalya climbed back onto the gravel road. With each quickened pace her resolve grew stronger.

"You can do this. You can make this work. You have to. You certainly aren't getting any younger."

She reached the front door just as Katherine opened it. There in front of her was her granddaughter clothed in sweatpants and an oversized sweatshirt Natalya had given her that belonged to her grandfather.

"Who were you talking to Memaw?"

Natalya smiled as she walked into the cottage. She took off her jacket and headed for the desk.

"Oh, just my inner conscious. It was in need of a pep talk."

Katherine stood in front of her grandmother with the sleeves of the sweatshirt engulfing her hands as she gave her grandmother a hug.

"I knew you could sort it out Memaw. I have some more reading to do so I'll say goodnight."

A gentle kiss was placed on Katherine's forehead and a pat on the butt as she turned and headed upstairs. Natalya reached out to the box on the shelf that now held most of the letters she had kept after the war. Still no email from Emily so she decided to sample her memory and read some more letters. She remembered when they simply dated the letters the month and year since their letters would take weeks and sometimes months to find them.

My Darling Natalya,   *June 1943*

I thought perhaps your letter got lost. At least I hope that is it. I am sorry that I offended you with reality. But it sounded from your letters like the beautiful sensitive Russian woman I knew and met in London was becoming a hardened, insensitive soldier oblivious to her surroundings!

There is so much cruelty that I have seen and experienced since I have been here. I couldn't possibly explain it in a letter. You were my one and only constant that reflected purity and love. Whenever I felt I could no longer take the horrors of this war I would think of you and the first time I met you with an arm full of books racing down the stairs of the nursing school.

> *I remember the gentleness you showed me when we collided. I remember nights before graduation that we spent huddled in your bed for warmth. Even when we went our separate ways, we still managed to have lunch at that old café on Bleaker street. And when I feel that all hope has left this godforsaken place, I remember our night in the Hotel Strasburg when we made love. The warmth of your skin and smoothness as you held me wave after wave of passion crossing both of our bodies.*
>
> *Did I dream all of that? Has this war finally turned the Natalya Ritenkoph into a monster? If so, did my Natalya die? My heart is heavy with this thought. Please forgive my directness. I hope you are well and I wish I could see you one last time.*
>
> *Love,*
> *Emily*

Natalya tried to remember what Emily was responding to. A small 3"x2" black and white photo fell from in-between the letters. It was a picture of Natalya and another woman brandishing a rifle in front of a plane. On the back was written '**My graduation from sniper school**"

She then remembered how energized she was after her first battle in the air. Each time she flew she felt as though she was in her element. Her commander ordering her to visit the hospital where her comrades were or else he would ground her? He made her feel like a misbehaving schoolgirl.

"Ahhh Natalya, you were truly an ass weren't you."

She picked up another letter that was dated before the last one she read. It seemed shorter than the ones she had been reading and it was in with a note from George stating it couldn't be delivered. Natalya figured since she wrote it, she could open it.

Dear Emily,   *April 1942*

I fear you will have to send our letters to your brother since I will be heading to Russia shortly for training. Stalin is forming an all-female combat unit and I can't wait to join. Funny how things work out. You will be fighting the Japanese whilst I will be fighting the Germans. This maybe the last secure letter I can send you before I leave. Miss our talks and evening meals together.

Love,
Natalya

So, Emily never knew where Natalya was sent to. She silently cursed her ex-husband George, as she put down the letter.

"All you had to do George was say you didn't want to forward our letters. We would have found another way."

She spoke under her breath. It was as if she hoped he would hear her. She moved the box over to the couch and sat with her legs up as she read more letters. Katherine padded down the stairs in her fuzzy slippers to see her grandmother asleep with letters all around her. Katherine picked up the letters, placed them back in the box and draped a blanket over her grandmother as she turned out the table lamp.

"Pleasant dreams Memaw"

And with that she placed another log in the fireplace, grabbed a glass of warm milk and headed back upstairs for some well needed sleep.

CHAPTER 8

Emily cursed under her breath as she looked for the letters she had squirreled away in a locker before she was sent to the Philippines. There weren't very many but they were like a life line when she came back from the war. Her brother sent her letters after she returned to California. It was shortly after that he told her of Natalya's death at the end of the war. She found one atop an ammo box she had kept from the war. It made a pretty secure mini locker for the items she wanted to keep safe. Her pins from the war she had long since removed from the leather bomber jacket Natalya gave to her. Those war time books given to soldiers on how to behave in other countries she kept merely for their humor. Since the American military was never prepared to have women in combat in other countries the books were given to soldiers stating how they were to act, especially with women. The humorous sections were when it discussed the various diseases one could catch from unknown women. Forget about what the soldiers brought. At least in Russia she figured that they were not given such books. From what Natalya told her their training was spent on reality and weather women could handle the required firearms.

Dear Emily,   *August 10, 1945*

Sniper training never prepared us for what we would see up close and personal. That perhaps is the difference between you and I. You see the results of war up close. The results of a sniper's bullet, the shrapnel of a bomb dropped by a plane or the results of a machine gunner are just some of the things you see. Perhaps it was a good thing for me to 'come down to Earth' as you said in your letter. We are preparing to land near one of the prison camps tomorrow.

Everyone here is hoping to liberate the thousands of prisoners Germany has there. I will obey my orders this time and stay with the plane. Had a difficult time seeing the horror of what the Germans had done. Small children still clutching their mothers' breast as they lay in shallow marked graves.

I try to listen for news of the war with Japan. We heard that they dropped something called an Atomic bomb on Hiroshima and they are fixing to drop another one in another location somewhere in Japan. Some of the officers say that they have never seen the type of destruction that this new bomb does to buildings and people. Some are saying it obliterates not only buildings but it evaporates them! Of course, that could just be typical war talk.

Hope to see you when the war ends if not before.

Love,
Natalya

Memories came flooding back as she read Natalya's letter . She remembered laying in her hospital bed as the news of the Japanese unconditional surrender came over the radio. Emily also remembered when she entered re-orientation briefly in Arkansas. The women nurses were told that whatever they did during the war should be kept to themselves. It was as if they wanted their service to simply disappear. PTSD (Post Traumatic Stress Syndrome) wasn't recognized when it came to nurses. Only men could be combat victims. Emily missed the nurses she served and suffered with. Those that survived after she was rescued suffered from Amoebic Dysentery and severe cases of Hepatitis. Damage to intestinal tracts, miscarriages and Depression were common.

Emily figured coming back to England would help her heal. But the hole that existed in her heart never got the chance to heal. For it was Natalya that Emily would think of when things got too rough. Even before the email, during full moons she would talk to Natalya and hope that her spirit would hear her. But now she was being given a second chance at closure. But the memories that went along with-it Emily wasn't too sure of. She remembered what she put her entire mothers' household thru when she returned from the war. The shrieking at night due to night terrors of starving bodies on surgery tables and the explosions that any flash of light would bring back put the entire household on edge. The drugs that were given to supposedly control these visions only made things worse to the point of becoming addictive. Her poor mother tried to help but was battling Cancer when Emily returned from the war. Finally, the neighborhood made up of her childhood friends banded together to take shifts to get her thru the addiction. Once the psychotropic drugs wore off, she gradually got better. After her mother was brought home after fainting on the factory floor Emily's issues became secondary. She dealt with those issues by caring for her mother. By the time her mother had passed, Emily was well on her way to recovery. But did she really want to relive all of that? She came across another letter. It was wrinkled and stained as more of the letters seemed to be getting.

Dearest Emily,

I miss you terribly. I am not sure if flying combat planes is worth all of this. We went from a 3-day hike in the hills to crossing the border in medical trucks to sneaking into a town in the dead of night so that we could volunteer in the morning with the rest of the men and women in town. Maybe I should have stayed with you in England. But the news states that Germany is not only moving thru France but bombing parts of England. Please be safe my love.

Till next time.
Love, Natalya

The letters, while disjointed in dates, brought back more memories both pleasant and not so pleasant. While she and Natalya were still in nursing school, she remembers the Japanese attack on the mainland near California. She looked at the date of the next letter. This one was from her brother George.

February 27, 1942
Dear Emily,

I fear no place is safe anymore. I have been assigned to the British office so I will be leaving California and will hopefully see you by the end of the month.

In case you didn't hear...the Japanese just blew up the oil refinery in Santa Barbara. Seems the war with Germany is heating up so keep your head down (laughing). Will check in with you when I get there.

George

Her brother was usually very matter of fact about things and was head of the household even before their father died. He was the one who would arrange their trips to the English countryside and made sure everyone's needs were met. When George finally enlisted, their father was becoming a regular at the local pub. George's brief tour of the states made him fall in love with California. He would talk of settling down there when his tour of duty was over. She was trying desperately to reconcile the brother she grew up with…with the images that his actions during the war were creating. How could he have told the two women that knew him, trusted him and had love for him that each was dead as a result of the war? Why such a lie? Her head was hurting as she tried to sort out the images she so carefully had filed away in her mind.

Emily took a break from sifting thru her ammo box for letters to sitting on the bench in her front yard. She watched from a distance as the tour busses lined up for the daily visit to the towns many spas. Even though most were salt springs the sulfur springs were the most popular. Luckily the wind never shifted for very long so the faint smell of sulfur never hung around much to repulse anyone. Emily watched as a bird flew by with a worm still wiggling from its beak. She followed it to a tall European Ash and a nest that was barely visible. She took a quick glance at her bird feeders full of seeds.

"Think that's my clue to have some lunch."

Emily returned inside and headed towards the kitchen. She chuckled as she looked at the inside of her fridge. A brief flashback to a small metal box called a fridge and a block of melting ice to keep everything cold instantly came to mind. The reminder to Natalya that it was her turn to secure the ice block from the iceman least they have no decent butter, which at the time was even more highly prized than meat. She blinked several times as if erasing that image.

"Think I'll have roast beef."

Emily now looked at her refrigerator that had a multi- tiered, well stocked variety of items. She looked down as she spoke to her very happy Welsh Corgi. As if on cue he went to his food bowl and grabbed a few kibbles of dog food. The teapot whistled as she finished constructing her sandwich.

"Perfect timing."

Emily grabbed a scone for her and a biscuit for Winston and sat down at the small breakfast nook she designed. Re-modeling her mothers' home to suit her needs was one of the first things she had pleasure doing. The second was choosing Winston from a neighbor's litter. The house seemed too empty after its makeover and the welsh Corgi named Winston seemed the perfect fit. She remembered Natalya's love of dogs and how Emily had to talk her out of getting an Irish Wolfhound puppy when they were in Nursing school. She knew Natalya had no idea how big Wolfhounds grew. She smiled as she ate her sandwich remembering the silly back and forth comments she and Natalya would exchange over the puppy. Winston curled up on Emily's feet as she drank her tea. Her thoughts were interrupted briefly by the house phone ringing. It was the local vet reminding Emily of Winston's vet check tomorrow.

"You're in trouble now boy."

He gazed up at Emily and sneezed as he laid his head back down. She propped her feet up as she sat in the window seat gazing out at her garden. Maybe this reconnection is for the better.

"Well boy? Think I'm doing the right thing by reconnecting with this woman?

Her Corgi simply looked at her as he cocked his head to one side. It certainly would be a test for her. A test to see if all of those demons from the war were truly under control.

CHAPTER 9

Katherine woke to the sounds of a barking dog as she tried to block the sun from her eyes. She was nice and warm under the covers but the sun was now filtering into her room. She suddenly realized who the barking dog was and threw the covers up on the bed.

"Barkley? Oh, my G-d it's Barkley!"

She quickly slid into her slippers, grabbed her bathrobe and hurried down the stairs. Katherine's grandmother was holding Barkley's leash when the two saw each other. With a yank of the leash the 120lb. Irish Wolfhound was off down the hall towards Katherine. Natalya squinted as she braced for the impact that was about to happen. Even as 130 lb. Katherine stood her ground the momentum of the 120 lb. wolfhound was no match and the two collided in the hallway amidst furious licking and a very hairy wagging tail.

"Did you have a good vacation Barkley?"

The two rolled about on the floor and re-arranged several carpets as Natalya walked over and held Barkley's favorite treat....an extra- large Milk Bone dog biscuit.

"If you two are finished dusting my hallway...I have an email to get back to."

The excited wolfhound sat perfectly still with only his tail creating swirls of hair as it moved.

"Okay...here you go. Good boy."

With that, the dog was off down the hallway to his very sizable doggy door and his fenced in area complete with a dog house that resembled a small shed and a good- sized water trough. He patrolled his fence line as he pranced around obviously happy, he was home. Natalya brought a breakfast tray out into the garden and placed it on the stone table that sat in the center. As Katherine laughed at Barkley's antics Natalya poured each a cup of tea. The two women sat down, sipped their tea and began to eat.

"Great eggs Memaw. How do you get them so fluffy?"

Katherine spoke as she shoveled in the food like a woman that had been starved. She put down her fork long enough to grab a slice of toast and spread some grape jam over it.

"Are we starving this morning? I just add a little cream as I am whipping them. Then I just pour the mix into the fry pan. It's really not rocket science. Glad you like them. But you might want to take a breath."

Natalya watched Katherine as she added a bit of the scrambled egg to her jellied toast. She remembered how Emily would sometimes make an egg sandwich doing the same thing. She smiled as she thought about Emily's combination breakfast sandwich. Grape jelly on one piece of toast, Strawberry jam on the other and the scrambled egg in the middle. Not to be outdone Natalya remembered adding cream cheese and bacon before the rationing began. Such a gourmet breakfast nothing could compare to. As she watched Katherine finally slow down, she noticed Barclay eyeing a squirrel.

"Barclay! Don't even think about it."

Natalya motioned for him to come to her. She was quite familiar with the stubbornness of Wolfhounds.

"Barclay! Now!"

Natalya's firm command got Barclay's attention and the squirrel was safe for now. The sun seemed reluctant to stay out and clouds made their way back above the cottage. As Katherine sipped her Earl Grey tea, she looked at her grandmother finishing her last bite of toast and smiling at Barclay's antics.

"Do you know if Emily has a dog? "

Natalya turned to face Katherine.

" You know, I don't know. I know that she loved dogs and we always had cats around our apartment in Nursing school. I'll ask next time I email her."

The two women finished breakfast. The sun was doing a random appearance peeking behind the clouds as the wind picked up slowly. Katherine remained outside with Barclay as Natalya went back inside to read more letters. She picked up a small photo of her old PO-2 plane. She had taken it to mail to Emily. She remembers how proud she was of getting her first plane. She remembered the plane being slow(around 94 mph vs 150 mph) but very maneuverable. She smiled as she closed her eyes and remembered her first flight. She could hear the whistle of the wind against the bracing wires as she flew above the Russian airfield. The canvas surface of the planes absorbed radar so they were virtually undetected plus they flew close to the ground which made them great for bombing runs. Her 110 hp engine generated very little heat for heat seeking equipment. For Natalya it was the perfect little plane. The other women pilots taught her a less evolved but very adrenaline causing maneuver during her second mission. She would cut her engine and silently glide towards the target. She would release her bombs, restart her engine then fly home. Other women thought that maneuver was too non direct and wanted to see the German pilot as they shot him out of the sky so they had a 7.62mm machine gun installed on a swivel where the observer's position would be. She was happy with her stealth method and she felt she was alive to this day because of it. In the fall of 1942, she trained in a much larger metal built anti-tank and ground attack plane. It needed a second crew member and had a rear machine gun. It was a faster plane and much sleeker looking. She was scheduled to fly over the Berezina River after the German invasion began. But they needed her flying expertise in her PO-2. Natalya remembered her being extremely arrogant as she listened to the other pilots complaining that they knew how to take off and land in the new Ilyusha-2's but not how to fire the guns or learn tactics of the plane. She remembered calling them cowards and that if she didn't have a mission with her PO-2 she would show them how to fly and fight with the new Il-2. Newspaper clippings within the chest showed how wrong she had been. In the first 3 days the 4th- ShAP squadron had lost 10 planes to enemy action. Some 20 pilots were killed and out of 65 planes that were manufactured that squadron only had 10 Il-2's by the end of 1941. After some retaining and development of anti-tank bombs many of her fellow pilots flew them on the Eastern Front attacking the Panther and Tiger tanks of Germany. But Natalya preferred her little mule PO-2. She loved flying aerial reconnaissance when she wasn't using her stealth technique for bombing raids against the Germans. If her granddaughter only knew. She smiled as she thought of her reaction. Natalya sat back in the sofa and propped her legs up as she drifted off to sleep.

Katherine picked up the photos that were scattered around her grandmother and placed a blanket over the now snoring woman. She glanced again at the photo of the plane and her grandmothers brilliant smile. She looked at all the different postmarks on the letters and wondered how those letters even found their way to the intended party. She figured it would be one more question to ask her Memaw when she awoke.

Natalya thought of how ironic it was that she flew planes in all those combat missions yet Emily who was a nurse on the ground was the one who became wounded by the war. Her dreams were of Emily reaching out to her wondering where she was. She had visions of her drinking with the other pilots while Emily laid in a hospital room alone and frightened. She woke up just as Katherine was putting the photos back into the box with the letters.

"Did you have a nice nap Memaw?"

Natalya yawned and stretched as she sat up. Realizing she was covered with a blanket she stood up to fold it and place it back on the couch.

"Nap yes, not too sure about nice. Maybe I'll do some more writing to Emily."

"Memaw? I have a question."

"Of course, child. What is it?"

"I've looked at all those postmarks and photos of all the places you traveled during the war."

"Yes?"

" How did those letters manage to find you?"

Natalya sighed as she sifted thru the letters.

"Well, some of them didn't. But for the most part you'd have to ask the 6888th CPD Battalion."

Katherine scowled as she looked at her grandmother. Natalya in turn laughed as she attempted to explain.

" Yes, I know…sounds like a mouthful but actually it stood for the Central Postal Directory Battalion. Apparently, it was made up of about 800 African American women from the Women's Army Corp, Army Service Forces and Army Air Force. Their motto was 'No mail, Low morale'. I met a couple of them when I was in England after the war. For me they were worth their weight in gold. I never wanted to be apart from Emily yet we could'nt possibly get any farther than where we were during the war. Yet I can't tell you how much getting one of her letters meant to me. I always held her letter close to my heart when it would arrive. Some of them I read over and over."

Katherine pulled out one of the more ragged, stained and partially singed ones. Even in its current state it looked as though it had been worn thin from the folding and unfolding and being carried against the skin.

"Some soldiers received battered cakes and crumbled cookies. But they didn't care. It was a connection to home. I remember one of the women who worked in the warehouse sorting letters…ahhh…I think her name was Carol, mentioning that the rats would try to get in to the mail because of the cookies and cakes."

"Ugh…that's gross!"

"Yes, it was. I remember when Carol and I walked to the warehouse since it was on the way to my apartment. Emily was still in the Philippines. That warehouse was colder inside than it was outside and it was snowing! She must have had like 3 layers of clothes on plus her wool Army coat. The mail bags were almost as high as the ceiling of the warehouse. When I commented about it, I remember her saying it was better than

it was. It definitely gave me a better understanding of how my letter was getting to Emily."

Katherine figured it was about time that she wrote down some of the notes she was forming in her brain as she listened to her grandmother. She gently kissed her on the cheek and went up to her room to get her laptop.

Natalya walked out to the garden and gazed out at the horizon. As the wind blew against her cheek she thought of her presence at that moment. She thought of the creaks and sounds her aging body made each day. She thought of the emptiness she felt when she was alone in the cottage. The nice cozy cottage with a King size bed that no one other than Barkley and her share. She would turn down reunions because it reminded her of Emily. She walked in the cottage and starred at the fireplace mantle with pictures of her daughter and granddaughter. She walked upstairs into her bedroom and there on the wall facing the bed were two 8x10 photos in 11x14 frames. One was of Natalya and Emily upon their graduation from nursing school. The other was a photo of Emily by the English seaside. Natalya then went up to the attic and opened the now familiar chest. Underneath a pile of old magazines were photos that her inquisitive granddaughter had missed. There was the small 3x5's and 5x7's photos of Emily. She even had the one that had her ex husband was cut out of. It showed her with Emily in front of a cottage in the Cottswalds. She then looked around and started rummaging thru boxes and file cabinets. Katherine heard the noise and popped her head in.

"What's up Memaw?"

"Can you help me find a box of small frames I had laying around here? They are left over from the ones I used on the mantle downstairs."

"Sure!"

The two women moved, lifted, sneezed and coughed their way around the attic until Katherine yelled.

"Found it! Ugh...I'm not sure I even want to know what that was."

Katherine pulled an old animal skeleton off the top of the tape sealed box. Natalya ripped open the box and pulled two handcrafted wood framed from the box.

"Ah...perfect!" "Here...let me clean those up for you. Where are these going?"

"Down stairs on the fireplace mantle."

"Okay, I'll meet you down there."

Katherine took the two frames and headed downstairs. Natalya carried the box into her bedroom and then went downstairs with the stack of photos . Katherine already had the two frames waiting. She had cleaned the glass and oiled the wood frames.

"Oh, these are lovely. Thank you my dear."

She sorted thru the photos and finally found the ones she had been looking for. The first one was of Natalya and Emily posing in front of an old jeep on the side of a road. The second was of Emily standing with a bouquet of flowers. It was one of the few that looked as though it had been colorized.

"Okay...why these two?"

"Well, this one of the two of us. It was taken by the side of the road when we had a flat tire and I had just finished changing it. Emily was going to take a picture of me changing the tire when this nice couple came along to see if we needed any help. The wife offered to take a picture of the two of us."

Natalya very carefully placed the photo within the frame and closed the back.

"And this one?"

Natalya took a moment as she looked at the photograph. Katherine watched as a smile gradually appeared on her grandmother's face.

"(sighing) This one is the one I took of Emily shortly after her orders came thru. We went and had lunch and I stopped by a field that had these beautiful yellow flowers. I picked a bouquet for her even though they made my nose itch. I didn't realize until later that it was a mustard field Emily was admiring. Your uncle who had that photo store in Chicago for a while colorized it for me. "

Katherine looked at the photo and could see the happiness on her grandmothers face as she looked at the photograph of her beloved Emily. Looking thru these photographs and letters Katherine was seeing another side of her grandmother. As she stood next to her she realized it was a gentler yet vulnerable side.

Natalya remembered that day as she sneezed her way back to the apartment with Emily. She smiled as she kept using her crumpled up handkerchief as she drove down the country road. Emily was desperately trying to be empathetic as she stifled, he giggles. It was an enjoyable day that made the women forget the hustle and bustle of the city and took them away from the constant talk of war and their possible deployment. Barclays vocal objection to a bird on his lawn brought Natalya back to the present.

"I'm going to scan this and send it to Emily."

Natalya turned and headed for her computer. As she scanned the photo she wondered if Emily would have the same fond memories as she did. The two women seemed to be perfect examples of opposites attracting.

"Hey Memaw.....I found this box with grandpas name on it. Do you know what's in it?"

Natalya briefly looked up. It was half the size of a chest box yet not as deep. She squinted as she looked above her glasses.

"Oh, that's your grandfathers' things from the military. I was going to give them to your mom."

"Do you mind if I have a look?"

Katherine said with a smile as her curiosity was in full bloom going thru the chest in the attic.

"No...of course not dear."

"Cool!"

Katherine sat on the couch and opened the box. A very musty odor filled her nostrils as she touched a very neatly folded uniform. Beneath it were several smaller boxes. Each one rattled as Katherine picked them up. Inside one was a Sterling Silver pocket watch that stopped at 4'oclock, a Masonic ring and a gold banded wedding ring. Upon opening up the next box she sneezed as the dust filled her nostrils and Natalya smiled.

"Don't tell me you can smell those mustard fields from there?"

Katherine wiped her nose with a tissue as she spoke.

"No...just a dusty box."

The smaller box held her grandfather's dog tags and 2 rather long bullets. On of the bullets had an engraving on it the brass of the bullet was slightly tarnished and somewhat faded. Katherine rubbed it on her shirt in an attempt to clean it. The name on the bullet was that of her grandmothers' Natalya. At first, she thought it was kind of neat. She continued to dig into the box. There were several letters that looked as though they had never been opened. They were addressed to her grandfather from headquarters in England. The envelope was old and the glue was dried & cracking. Katherine slid her long fingernail in between the flap and carefully opened the letter.

June 1941

Dear Lieutenant Winthrop,

As per your request, Nurse Emily Winthrop has been reassigned to Fort Stotsenberg Station Hospital in the Philippines.

Have placed Natalya Ritenkoph on the AWOL list and her name does not appear on any pilots lists we have received. You might want to check with Engels School of Aviation north of Stalingrad.

Remember those cigars can be left with my Sgt. Major Croft. Hope to see you when this war is over for that drink you owe me.

Your Fishing Buddy,
Commander Davidson

Katherine tried to process what the letter meant.

"Memaw? What does AWOL mean?"

Natalya briefly looked up a bit puzzled at her granddaughters' question.

"It's the military's abbreviation for Absent Without Leave. Meaning the soldier wasn't given permission to leave the base or barracks. He was in trouble and risked getting kicked out of the military or court martialed."

Katherine placed the box down and brought the letter over to her grandmother.

"I think you should read this?"

Katherine's tone was somber as she placed her hand on her grandmothers' shoulder. Natalya read the first paragraph and was confused. She read the second paragraph and became angry. Pearl Harbor wasn't attacked until December 1941.

"That bastard!"

Natalya turned to face Katherine.

"Why did grandpa want to get you in trouble?"

Natalya scrunched the letter and then threw it down on the desk. She then cupped Katherine's face as she spoke.

"I never knew he did this. I was already heading over to Russia to start my training. I wasn't assigned to any nursing station or military post. I could have headed back to the states if I wanted to. I already had my flight training from those flight training schools in Texas and California. It was before we received military ranking. As for why the bastard did it ...well... he must have been jealous and wanted us apart. I can't believe he would have intentially placed Emily , his sister, in harms way? After all, according to the date of this letter Pearl Harbor hasn't been attacked yet. See? The letter is dated June 1941.

Natalya pushed her chair away from the desk as Katherine stood up. She was desperately trying to make sense out of the letter. She knew how George felt about her when she was around Emily. He flirted with her and would tease her about her hair. It was starting to make sense of why he lied to her about Emily being dead. He loved being in control and loved that Emily entrusted her letters to him. Even though she says he never opened them Natalya was beginning to have her doubts.

"Hey Memaw...your bomber jacket fits me!"

Natalya turned to see Katherine in her flight jacket. She had an instant flashback to the day she received hand me down Russian uniforms and oversized boots to stand up to the snow at Engels. She remembered the older pilots showing her how to tear up their bedding to stuff into her boots so they would fit. Flying at night, her hand me down uniforms had to endure and protect her from freezing temperatures, wind burn and frostbite. She welcomed that bomber jacket that seemed to now dwarf Katherine. Katherine could see the confusion on her grandmothers' face. Katherine thought a diversion would work.

"So, tell be about this bomber jacket?"

"So tell me about this Bomber Jacket?"

Katherine glided her hands across the worn leather at her grandmother spoke.

"Oh that's my second one. I gave the one I had from my flight school to Emily0 before I left for France."

Natalya sat back down looking out the window as she spoke.

"Once I got smuggled into Russia the weather was absolutely horrible. Well, our planes were so cold just touching them could rip your skin off. So, we lit fires alongside of them to warm the surrounding air temperature. That jacket was warm and kept my upper body from getting frostbite. What you didn't know was that we didn't have parachutes. The cockpits were so small they would never fit a parachute. We didn't have radar, radios or guns. We communicated with flashlights."

Katherine looked puzzled.

"But if you didn't have radar or radios how did you do your mission?"

Natalya smiled and sat down next to Katherine.

"We used rulers, stop watches, maps and compasses. We could virtually plot a course anywhere! You see, our planes were slower than the stalling speed of those Nazi planes which made our planes harder to target. We could also take off and land in very small clearings."

Katherine could see the pride and joy on her grandmothers face when she talked about those planes she flew.

"But what about the negatives of your plane?"

Natalya paused before she spoke. Familiar words were about to be said for a second time in her life.

"Huh...When the enemy fired it was hard to duck so we would put the plane into a dive. Our planes had no defense devices either. We could only carry two bombs at a time. And when our planes were hit by tracer bullets their explosive charge would ignite our wooden planes. Whoosh! Up in flames we'd go. See...the first plane would act as bait. They would attract the Germans spotlight. Then I would idle my engine and glide into the bombing area. They couldn't hear us coming so we could bomb a lot of their high value targets. It was glorious. It was said that some of those Nazi soldiers called us witches on wooden broomsticks."

Her grandmother let out a hearty laugh as she felt the arm of the bomber jacket. Katherine couldn't remember the last time she saw her grandmother so happy. Natalya got up and went to the window. Her brain was cluttered with images of her husband, Emily and the missions she flew. Reading that letter and thinking of Emily stirred an emotion she thought she had lost...love. She loved Emily and when she was told she died she never found anyone who could fill the hole in her heart. It had been some 55 years that Natalya chose to live by herself in Maine with only her dog Barclay and an occasional visit from her daughter and granddaughter. Maybe it was about time she set things straight and visited her long lost only love. She cautioned herself not to get too caught up in that emotion since she was in no mood to get hurt again. She walked back towards Katherine.

"What would your mother say to a little trip to Europe? My treat."

Katherine looked up with a big smile. She walked over to her grandmother and spoke.

"I still have my passport from when my class went to Cancun last year. I'm not sure she would be too pleased though. She would want to know why I guess."

Natalya stood defiant as she spoke.

"You leave your mother to me. Seems to me she owes me one. Which I will definitely remind her of. "

The next day saw a flurry of activity within the Ritenkov household. Barclay ran about the house chasing Katherine as she ran up and down the stairs adding things to her suitcase.

"Are you sure I can only bring one grandma?"

Natalya smiled as she placed one medium suitcase next to Katherine's rather large bulky suitcase. While it was square and quite large it had no rollers and Natalya could just see them trying to navigate that suitcase down an escalator.

"What on earth do you have in there? How many clothing changes do you think you could possibly need? You are going to have a hell of a time navigating that thru a crowded airport. Here! Use this one. Try and get all your clothes in this one."

Natalya gave Katherine a medium sized suitcase with rollers and then proceeded to show her how to fold her clothes military style so she might have room for everything she packed which seemed to be most of the same thing: t-shirts, jeans and underwear.

"Here! The taxi will be here shortly. I'll leave you to it."

A knock on the door sent Barclay downstairs and barking behind Natalya.

"What a great protector you are."

Natalya laughed as she opened the door and then smiled as the pet-sitter strolled in.

"Christina! Long time no see."

Both women laughed since she was the one who also groomed Barclay.

"Okay, the fridge is fully stocked and the cable is paid up thru the end of the month. We will check in on you from time to time in the late evenings due to the time difference. Thank you again for doing this on such short notice."

Natalya then handed her an envelop with some cash in it . Barclay came over to greet Christina as she pet his head and ears. She was a retired veterinarian who had been injured one too many times while working with horses. She found pet sitting with a few wealthy clients just as rewarding and allowed her to spend time designing jewelry which was her passion. Just then the taxi pulled up and gave several honks.

"Okay Katherine, that's our cue. Thank you again Chris."

Natalya hugged Chris as Katherine bounded down the stairs with her new rolling suitcase. She also had a very bulky backpack strapped to her back which made her look like she was about to tip over. Both Christina and Natalya chuckled as she handed her luggage to the taxi driver. They both waved goodbye as Christina held on to Barclay's harness.

"How did you ever get mom to agree to this trip?

Natalya checked her passport as she spoke to Katherine.

"I simply reminded her of a small indiscretion that I helped her with. When I started to recall the particulars, she stopped objecting.

Katherine then smiled as she too took her passport from her jacket pocket making sure it was stamped.

"And let me guess...you are not going to tell me what that indiscretion was are you?"

With a smile the two women gazed out the taxi window as they headed towards the airport.

CHAPTER 10

Emily was a bit perturbed by the phone call from Natalya that basically said she was coming for a visit and would let her know when they had arrived. She had resolved many of the issues she had throughout the years regarding her self-imposed seclusion from the outside world. She had made peace with the demons from her POW days. But her relationship with Natalya was the one thing she didn't think she would have to deal with ever again. She was alive! After her brother informed her of Natalya's death, she remembered the thoughts of suicide that she had to deal with and the years of mourning that followed. She remembered how tired she was of people trying to put a time limit on her mourning the woman she loved. She finally went to therapy to deal with all of these emotions so she could start to sleep again.

Now, within the span of several weeks all these feelings were returning with the mention of Natalya being alive. Without realizing it she had gone up to the attic of her home. There in the corner sat a large footlocker. She sighed as she walked over and opened it. She starred momentarily at the neatly pressed nurses uniform that sat atop neatly wrapped books, packages and photo albums. The sound of her dog's license tags as he scratched his collar brought her back to reality. As she removed her folded uniform and scanned the labeled photo albums she wondered if she wasn't opening a can of worms by looking thru her "War Trunk" as she called it. She found the album she was hunting for. As she placed everything back within the trunk, she glimpsed her reflection in an old, dusty, round rotating floor mirror. How old she seemed to have gotten. She carefully moved her fingers around the outlines of her scarred face. The disfigurement reminder caused her to look away. It seemed only yesterday that she looked into that very mirror to celebrate an award ceremony for the medal she received many years after the war.

As she slowly descended the stairs with the album in hand she wondered again if seeing Natalya was such a good idea. While it sounded weird to let someone remain "Buried" after you found they were alive, Emily remembered the years of therapy she went thru to deal with her time as a POW and then the therapy to deal with Natalya's death. She sat down in front of the large picture window facing the garden. The Lilacs and America Beauty Roses were in full bloom as the yellow mustard fields framed the background. Emily had the old family house remodeled after the war to reflect a more open floorplan. Large picture windows were present throughout the house and even the bathrooms had large glass block and skylights to reflect a more open-air feeling.

A picture fell out of the album as Emily bent over to catch it. It was a sketch that Natalya had done of her plane she was flying for the Russian military. Natalya would sketch her little scenes at the end of some of the poems she would send her.

Isn't she beautiful.

She remembered the letter that accompanied it. She was so happy about flying while Emily thought about her being a target in the air. As Emily went thru the black & white photos of the war, she started to get an upset feeling in the pit of her stomach. She decided that a glass of rum over ice was better than an antacid. So, she poured herself a double and sat back down to the photo album. Emily's dog Winston curled up beside her as she opened the album. She smiled as she remembered the months of therapy and the final week when she was ready to sort thru the box of photos to place into an album. Her therapist suggested that as her new mission, she should place the photos in albums much like a scrapbook. It would help her in the healing process.

The Japanese were always taking photos of the camps and nurses to use in their propaganda films. Emily managed to get one of those cameras when the camp was liberated. By the time she was ready to begin her photo album she had well over 200 photos . The opening page had a photo of Emily's nursing school in London and her photo of the teachers. As she turned the page there was the youthful photo of Natalya bandaging another student. It was a rather humorous one since the student looked more like a mummy than a patient. Since Emily and Natalya hung out in a group of four other girls there were all sorts of funny photos of the group eating, playing and studying. But the photos always seemed to catch Natalya casting an eye towards Emily. She always felt that Natalya had a presence that exuded confidence and maturity. Maybe it was her Russian upbringing. Emily was never sure but she knew that if Natalya was behind it would succeed. As she turned the pages of memories, she had to admit that her favorite photo was the one of Natalya in her bomber jacket and aviator glasses standing in front of her plane. She always saw Natalya as very sexy in that photo. She liked it so much she had an 8x10 replica on her nightstand. She looked up and caught her reflection in a 11x14 frame of her parent's farm. She traced once again the scarring from being burned during her rescue from Corregidor. It practically covered the entire side of her face. She quickly closed the album.

"Oh, good Lord. This is insane! What do you think you are doing? This will never work."

She spoke out loud and looked at her Corgi as if expecting confirmation. She threw the album towards the end of the sofa got up and headed outside to get some air. As she walked down the path, she looked up overhead as a commercial plane flew into the clouds. It was as if she were transported back to the fields near Dover where she waited for Natalya as she ferried one of the new bombers to be used in the war. Remembering the flight, they had shortly after seemed as clear in her memory as the day it happened. Natalya wanted to do more and Emily wanted her to be with her. While the Blitzkrieg had started in London the neighboring villages were where some of the nurse's stations had been set up and were free from the constant shelling. After Natalya landed, they drove to the town in silence. Before dinner Emily tried once again to convince Natalya to stay with her while she worked at the nurse's station. But once again an argument ensued. Instead of spending a night together making love, Natalya spent it on the couch and Emily crying in the bed. The following morning Natalya left Emily a note apologizing but telling her she wanted to do more for the war effort. She would try and enlist with the Russian flight school since they were actively flying their planes into battle utilizing both men and women. She explained how she would try to get across enemy lines either by way of the underground or by some smuggling method. Emily ripped up the letter but taped the pieces back up after her anger subsided. A neighbor honked at Emily as they drove by. Emily looked around and realized she had walked quite a distance from her home. She turned around and thought about the time their car ran out of petrol and they wound up walking several miles before having to do a 12-hour shift. She walked back to her house and picked up the album once more.

Emily laughed as her fingers ran over the photos jogging memories of Natalya. As she closed the album midway, she allowed her heart to feel a certain emotion she thought she had long since lost...love. They were both different women. So much time and pain had passed and been dealt with. Was it really worth it to dredge it all up again? She placed the album down on the sofa and went back upstairs to the attic. As she dug further down, she found what she was looking for. There in a neatly wrapped lavender ribbon were the poems Natalya had written and sent to Emily shortly before the war. She walked back down to the sofa and sat down as she untied the ribbon.

Lady in The Tower

Like a knight who is scaling a tower
For the damsel in distress
You have no doors that are open
Only walls that seem to compress

They compress as I lay here beside you
They compress as I touch your soft skin
They compress as you get up and smile
Yet they still won't let me in

You state that your fear is the cause for the tower
And an entrance does truly exist
But your walls bar the entrance and have me confused
Should I kiss you or wait to be kissed

How do I reach you-----Oh Lady in the tower?
When the bricks have been so carefully rearranged
Do I patiently wait in this garden of roses?
Or watch as my armor rusts in the rain

My call as a knight compels me
To be honorable, chivalrous and true
But my patience is like that of a woman in love
Desperation will finally push through.

Emily remembered when they toured the museum and Natalya looked at the armor and swords. She recalled later that evening Natalya saying she wanted to be her 'knight in shining armor'. It was shortly after that when they had a split shift and Emily came home to the apartment to find this poem resting on her pillow. She pulled out another that appeared to have been crumpled up then pressed out.

Why are you so selfish?
Every time we talk
Are you just not listening?
Or do you like to walk

Walk out on my feelings
Where carefully I tread
Where no one shares much interest
With all the things I've said

Why are you so selfish?
Every time I hurt
Are you so conditioned?
Or do you practice being curt

Why are you so selfish?
When depression we all share
Are you the only one here?
Who really seems to care?

Is it really so hard for you to share?
In my happiness and enthusiastic thought
To help decorate the apartment for the season
And not feeling like you've been caught

With every word that Emily read the memories returned like the dusty pages of a favorite book. Natalya was so passionate about certain things and Emily use to find it amusing when she would seem to get so upset when Emily wasn't on the same page. Natalya wanted to move out of their tiny apartment since her parents had sent her money. She was tired of walking up the 12 flights of stairs and tired of the plumbing not working and a host of other things. The apartment was tiny and you could hear the conversations of others thru the walls not to mention the lack of hot water or sometimes water at all. Emily pulled out another letter not wanted to end on a negative memory. This one was on the bottom of the stack and seemed to be lightly scented.

Moonlight Dreams

We kissed in the calmness of moonlight
Held tight in the warmth of embrace
Surprised in the calmness and comfort
That both of our bodies displayed

Fearful of going much further
Neither one of us wishing to stop
Held each other at a safe distance
As our eyes grew intensely locked

We will have all the time later
As we smiled and agreed with the clock
That the warmth and emotion
That we now were feeling
Would continue and never stop

It won't stop at the work place that morning
Nor the sanctuary you call home
The feeling that came and haunts you each hour
Will only continue to roam

As you wait for the peace that awaits you
The moon starts to rise and glow
And the lover that kissed you
The evening before
Returns to your dreams once more

Emily suddenly felt a warmth and used the letter as a fan as she attempted to cool herself down. This poem Emily remembered all too clearly. The two of them had driven to the countryside and stayed with a friend. Wanting to get some privacy, later that evening Natalya had put some wine in a thermos, grabbed a wool blanket and walked with Emily to a small wooded section that over looked a cliffside. She had taken a lantern but it wasn't used because of the beautiful full moon that was out. She realized she was blushing after reading the poem. She sighed as she looked at the letters and the photo album. Was it simple nostalgia or was Emily trying to avoid living in her past. Emily looked around the room. She realized that her décor reflected a period frozen in time. When she returned from the war her parents left her their ancestral home complete with 40's and 50's wallpaper, furniture and paintings. While Emily did her best to update the home it still had the feel of the 50's. She looked around and shook her head.

"Good lord Winston! It's the 90's and you would think I'd be able to get with the program. This is my home not my parents. It's definitely time for an upgrade."

She looked down at Winston as he cocked his head at her and wagged his stubby hind end. She called in a few favors from her friends at an antique shop in London. Emily knew that the money she would get from selling the Indian rugs that were throughout the home would more than pay for the painting and new furniture. There was even a dealer who took interest in some of her furniture when she hosted a yearly open house. Emily wasn't sure when Natalya was to arrive but she convinced herself that she was doing this for herself and not to impress her guest.

The next day Emily's house was a torrent of activity. The painters came to access the workload, show Emily swatches of pastel colors and discuss fees. Her friends Marge and Frankie from the antique shop came and were moving furniture and rolling carpets as

Emily sat in her garden drinking her tea. Marge came over and placed a gentle hand on Emily's shoulder.

"Are you sure about all this? We've been trying to get you to do this for ages."

Emily poured Marge a cup of tea.

"Yes, it's time for a fresh start. I've been living in the 40's for too long. It's about time to start living in the present."

Marge sat down next to Emily and watched the birds as the sun crested over the trees.

CHAPTER II

Natalya was happy to finally sit down even if it was on the plane. She took the window seat as Katherine settled in next to her. While everyone else nervously gripped the armrests, Natalya's attention was drawn to the approaching clouds. The clutter of the Earth gave way to the freedom and expanse of the clouds. Natalya could now at last relax and get some well needed sleep for the 12-hour flight. Katherine looked over and saw her grandmother asleep. She thought about the past few days being a blur as she realized how a simple search revealed such an adventure. She also realized that after this incident her telling her mother about moving into an apartment wouldn't be such a big deal or so she hoped. She reached for a book and thought about how irritated her mother must be at her traveling to England. She hoped she was doing the right thing since she would never forgive herself if her grandmother wound up being hurt. She smiled as she settled in to her book.

Natalya dreamt of flying thru the clouds and gliding down towards the targets as her navigator readied the bombs to be dropped. She remembered the arguments Emily and she use to have in their letters. So much time passed between letters that it was difficult to stay angry. All these years of loneliness that could have been spent with Emily. When she thought about how George had lied to her the anger returned. She thought about how he treated her during their marriage. She was a conquest, something to be controlled. The sex was especially rough. It was as if he wanted to make her submit by drilling himself into her.

As much as she would try to ease him into it his action would always be the same. He would grab her arms, pin her to a wall or the bed and have his way with her. She would soak for hours in hopes of relieving the soreness and sometimes pain between her legs. Several times his bite marks on her body had to be treated. He would never place them where others could readily see them. Being a doctor, he was clever that way. Even after his death when Natalya tried dating, she would have difficulty having sexual relations. After her first date with a man she realized the times were slowly changing and she could date women a bit more openly than before. But even then she would have flashbacks at the most inappropriate times. The woman she was in bed with usually heard Natalya call out Emily's name more than once. That usually ended the 1st date and definitely was a guarantee that there would be no 2nd date. The plane descended and jogged Natalya awake. She was surprised that she slept so soundly. 5 hours had passed and she was starting to get hungry. As she looked over at Katherine who was sound asleep, she saw the stewardess starting to roll down the aisle with food trays.

"Katherine dear, time for dinner."

Natalya gently nudged her granddaughter awake as a sirloin steak, baked potato and peas wafted past her nose. Katherine had a soda while Natalya had an iced tea. The cabin was buzzing with noise from glasses clanking to people getting up and stretching. Natalya ordered a Whiskey Sour and gazed back out at the window. Katherine talked to her about everything from boyfriends, girlfriends to courses and her outlook on her future. Natalya wished she had built a better relationship with her daughter Lianna. She never meant to ignore Lianna but before her therapy she looked at Lianna as a constant reminder of her involvement with George. After many months of therapy, she realized her issues had nothing to do with the war. Her issues were with George and her relationship with Emily. She was married to George but never felt comfortable . After therapy she came to terms with being a Lesbian and having a better relationship with her daughter Lianna.

Natalya got up and headed to the upstairs bar. It was the only thing she approved of in the modern passenger planes. Several men of various ages were already around the crescent shaped bar. Several young women were seated at a table by a window. She ordered something a bit smoother which ,to her was Bourbon over ice. She sat down at an empty table near the stairs. She thought back on all the times after she had finished a mission, she would invite her mechanic and copilot for a drink. She never thought until now that it was a celebration of making it back alive for one more mission. Her thought was interrupted by a waitress holding a Cognac glass half full of an amber liquid.

"The gentleman with the beard thought you could use something a bit more classy."

Natalya scowled at his pickup line and looked at the waitress. She had beautiful green eyes and a brilliant smile.

"Is that the best pickup line he could come up with?

The waitress laughed as she placed the glass down. Natalya thought about refusing the drink but Cognac at $20.00 a glass of Courvoisier VS she thought better of it. While she was flattered by the gesture, she would have been happier if the ladies had sent it to her. She smiled at the man and sipped the amber liquid. It had a rich bouquet of woody notes. Smooth flavors of spice, Almond and Cinnamon blended with the delicate taste of ripe fruits made the dink most pleasurable. She always did love good Cognac. She wasn't in the mood for small talk and luckily Katherine finally came up and sat down next to Natalya.

"Glad you showed up. A man at the bar bought me a drink."

Katherine wasn't sure if she liked that idea or not . She was about to say something when the waitress came over.

"He even had a really bad pickup line. She knows."

As Natalya pointed to the waitress she smiled and winked at Natalya. As she took Katherine's soda order Natalya noticed the waitresses gold necklace, a Lambda.

"So, are you nervous about meeting Emily after all this time?"

Natalya leaned back in her chair as she sipped her Cognac.

"A little I suppose. I'm still trying to process why your grandfather told such a lie. Emily and I probably would have been living happily ever after with each other. I remember wanting to search for her and bring her body back home. I thought your grandfather would go thru the roof. He started yelling and threw several glasses on the floor."

Natalya slid her chair closer to Katherine's as she spoke.

"You know, I always thought his behavior odd. I mean after all…this was his sister we were talking about. You would have thought he had a bit more compassion."

Katherine drank her Pepsi as she listened to her grandmother.

"To think of all those years apart. And then there's her accident. I couldn't even be there for her."

Katherine placed her hand over her grandmothers and caressed it gently.

"I'm sure she missed you as well."

Natalya patted Katherine's hand.

"Yes, but I can just imagine the horrors and pain she had to endure as a POW. After all, I remember the camp we liberated in Germany. It was truly horrible. I use to think after everyone was removed that the camp should have been leveled to the ground. After being with your mom I realized why it should have remained as we found it. That way the next generation could see what happened there. Maybe once they saw it, they would not let it happen again."

The warmth of the Cognac was getting to her. She padded Katherine on the shoulder and told her she was going back to her seat to take a nap. Katherine went down with her since she did not want to be alone in the bar. Katherine figured she could finish her book since the 12 hour flight was only halfway across the Atlantic.

Natalya and Katherine fell asleep and awoke to the *"fasten seatbelt"* sign indicating that they were about to land. It was a surprisingly smooth landing considering it was such a large plane. One they went thru customs and security Natalya hailed them a taxi to take them to their hotel.

"Hotel Barclay please."

Katherine's mom took her to a 4-star hotel once and she thought it was quite fancy. This hotel was a 5-star and definitely paled in comparison. After the bellhop opened the room and showed them where everything was located, she watched Natalya tip him and locked the door.

"Oh Memaw…this is spectacular!"

Katherine went to the window and gazed out onto the hussle and bustle of the city of London and a partial view of the River Thames at night.

"Since it's so late I'm going to order room service. Here ...pick what you want."

Natalya handed Katherine the menu of the 24-hr. room service. She opted for a salad, some rolls and a pitcher of ice tea. Natalya thought that sounded good and made it a double. After dinner Natalya went for a walk. Katherine showered and retreated to her very fluffy bed that she literally sank into.

Natalya walked down to the lobby and out towards the pool area figuring she would get the lay of the land during the day tomorrow. Until then it was safer to stay within the hotel grounds. She figured it was too late to call Emily so she would text her tomorrow. She started to wonder if she was doing the right thing. The wall she had always kept up was starting to crumble. Time apart had caused them to both become independent people. If Natalya's relationships were any indication then no one quite measured up. Each relationship Natalya had after the war was always missing something. Her eyelids were getting heavy. She went back up to the room to find Katherine snoring. She chuckled as she undressed. After her shower the bed was a welcomed feeling. Even with Katherine's snoring Natalya fell asleep as soon as her head hit the pillow.

The morning sun peeked around the drapes as Natalya got up first and stretched. Her bones creaked and the soreness of certain muscles returned. She pulled the drapes across the window like one would rapidly pull a band aid from a wound.

"Rise and shine granddaughter. Time to get dressed and do breakfast."

Natalya smacked Katherine on the rump as she looked up Emily's phone number in her little pad she carried. Her daughter use to call it her little black book since it was always filled with women's numbers and addresses. Katherine threw the covers off as she managed to sit upright on the bed. Natalya had to smile as she looked at Katherine hair. It looked like a beehive and on top was a bird's nest.

"You might want to start with your hair. Unless you are intentionally smuggling a baby bird in it."

Katherine made a grumpy face as she disappeared into the bathroom with her luggage. Natalya chuckled as she finished dressing.

Once the two women went down and were seated at a table by the window, Natalya asked for Katherine's phone.

"Well, I might as well get this over with. I'm going to go out there and call Emily. Order me the usual will you please."

Katherine handed her the phone and looked Natalya in the eye.

"It will be okay Memaw. Just breathe."

She smiled as the waiter came over to take her order. Natalya walked out towards the pool area and sat down under a canopy. She shakily opened her book to the page she had dogeared earlier. She dialed the number and swallowed. She then cleared her throat. After several rings the phone picked up.

"Hello? Emily? It's Natalya. Natalya Ritenkoph."

The minute Natalya spoke she felt foolish. Of course, Emily knows your last name she thought.

"Good morning! How are you? Where are you? Sorry... there's a lot of noise going on. Let me step outside for a moment."

Natalya waited quietly as she strained to listen to the other end of the line.

"There …that's better. So, are you in London?"

Natalya answered and went on to explain where they were staying and she had planned to show her granddaughter a few tourist sites and then maybe make arrangements to see Emily if that was possible. A long silence was felt. Natalya swallowed as she waited for Emily to respond.

"I actually would love to get away from this racket. Could I possibly persuade you two to come up here? We have a rather nice inn and I could show you the sites here. I'm not sure I'm ready for a public showing just yet but here the townspeople know me and don't really care about my looks."

Natalya was excited about the prospect of being with Emily for longer that a brief dinner. She wasn't sure about Emily's "looks" and started for the first time to wonder how bad the scar was. Katherine and she could play tourist at the end of their stay instead so Natalya readily agreed.

"That sounds awesome actually. So, let me write down the information for the inn and I'll…."

Emily interrupted her and Natalya flagged down a hotel pool person with a pen.

"Oh, I can take care of the reservations for you if you like. That way you just have to get a rental car."

Emily seemed much more efficient than Natalya remembered. She agreed and told her she looked forward to it. Emily would make her reservation at the inn for later in the afternoon giving Natalya plenty of time to navigate a rental car. She got off the phone and stared at the rippling water of the pool. It was as if she were trying to get in touch with flood of emotions her body was feeling. She handed back the pen and headed back in for breakfast and to tell Katherine of the new plans.

Luckily, Natalya still had her European Driving License from her travel days so renting a car was not as difficult as she anticipated. The rental car was a little Grey SUV that still had that new car smell as Katherine pointed out. The two women loaded their luggage into the small vehicle and Natalya navigated their way out of London and onto the M1 motorway. This was the 1st of the inter urban motorways. The GPS unit placed their arrival in 4 hours.

As they traveled past the various small towns Natalya remembered certain areas of the countryside that she flew planes from before she ran off to join the Russian female pilots.

"This area here past Coventry use to be the 12th group Fighter Command. We would fly out towards the North Sea and then towards Belgium. Never engaged in combat. Just ferry planes from one area to the other."

Natalya's smile disappeared as some other negative memories returned.

"Memaw? Why did you love flying so much?"

She could see that her grandmother needed a distraction. She could see her sigh as she answered.

"It's a feeling of total freedom. You're almost floating below the clouds and then thru them. Just a very unique feeling. Besides, hasn't there ever been something you feel so strongly about that you would do almost anything to do it?"

Katherine thought a moment as she looked out at a sign labeled Aylesbury.

"Well, yes actually. But you have to promise not to say a word to mum."

Natalya smiled and felt privileged that her granddaughter would trust her with, what obviously was a secret.

"Promise!"

Katherine turned to face Natalya as she adjusted her seatbelt.

"I've been saving for a down payment for an apartment after graduation. Mum seems to think I'm going to stay with her forever. I've already got a position as a Photojournalist with a magazine when I graduate. But mum thinks it's only temporary. They've offered me a full-time job after graduation and have a contract for me to sign and everything. I've tried talking to her about it but we just wind up arguing."

Natalya sighed as she revealed how difficult her daughter could be if you disagreed with what she herself wanted.

"Yes, well I might be partially to blame for that. You see, when your mum lived with me, I kept wanting her to go live her life when she turned 18 but she only wanted to stay with me. We use to have a really good relationship and then we started arguing constantly about how she really needed to get out and find her way. She use to say when she had a children, she would never want them to leave. So, you see...it's kind of a Déjà vu thing for her. I'm sorry you are bearing the brunt of that emotion. I suppose if you wanted me to, I could talk to her."

Katherine turned back to face the windshield.

"Its okay. I'll handle um. At least now I know what's behind it."

After an hour and a half of driving Natalya stopped in Northampton so they could stretch their legs while they enjoyed the grassland and wetland bird habitats of Barnes Meadow Nature Preserve. Natalya breathed in the air as Katherine took photographs. After a short respite the two women were off in the car once more. The radio played music while each woman seemed deep in thought.

Hours passed as Natalya was feeling the effects of both a long drive and constant memories. Finally, a sign for Harrowgate appeared to her left. She looked over as Katherine was sound asleep with her head cushioned with her jean jacket propped against the cars window. She lowered the radio and pulled off the motorway. The GPS signaled they were only 20 minutes from their destination. Natalya breathed a sigh of relief as she pulled into the parking lot of the inn.

While Katherine woke up, Natalya went to check in. Just as Emily had promised there was a reservation for two waiting. She walked back out to the car as Katherine was pulling the luggage from the boot of the car.

"Second floor, Rooms 7 & 8 "

Natalya held out two silver skeleton keys. She helped Katherine as she struggled with the suitcases. She tried to quietly roll them up the carpeted stairs and she held onto the bannister. Both women collapsed onto the bed once Natalya opened the door to her room.

"Do you want this room?"

Katherine sat up and looked at the single bed.

"Let's see the other room, shall we?"

Katherine unlocked the door to the adjoining room. It had the feel of an old wooden ship. Dark wood and old paintings decorated the rooms as if they were frozen in time. Katherine smiled at her grandmother with a devilish grin.

"Flip you for it?"

Natalya smiled as she threw a well-aimed pillow at her granddaughter.

"Well, the Chauffer is tired so I'm going to get some rest."

Natalya handed her the key and headed back to her room which was identical to Katherine's.

Both women took their shoes off and got comfortable. Both slept until Natalya was awakened by the phone next to her bed.

"Hello? Yes , the rooms are wonderful. Thank you so much for the reservation. No, that's fine. I guess we will see you at breakfast. Thank you again."

Emily had recommended a pub around the corner from the inn for dinner. Natalya splashed water on her face as she opened up the connecting door a bit wider. Katherine was changing her shirt as she looked up.

"Emily called. We will meet her for breakfast tomorrow at 10 am. For now, she said there's a pub around the corner for dinner. Are you hungry?"

Katherine smiled tied her shoes and grabbed her jean jacket.

"Are you kidding? I'm famished!"

The two women headed off to dinner.

CHAPTER 12

The sun peered thru the curtains of Natalya's room as she turned over. Her alarm had been set for 7 and as she checked her watch, she knew she should get moving. She had 5 minutes before her watch started its familiar chime. Natalya showered and chose her black jeans and salmon colored Polo shirt. As she dressed the butterflies in her stomach began. She hadn't experienced these since the first meeting of her granddaughter at age 9. Her daughter never seemed to want the two together but since she was going away on assignment and needed to leave Katherine with someone she reluctantly agreed to the meeting. When the two met it was as if they had always been together. Katherine hugged her grandmother and followed her everywhere. She listened to her grandmother tell her stories and asked relatively intelligent questions afterwards. It always made Natalya smile. She was more attentive to her granddaughter as if making up for her strained relationship with her daughter.

Sounds were stirring from the adjoining room as Natalya finished tying her hiking boots. She knocked on the door as she opened it to Katherine fully dressed and humming as she listened to her air pods.

"Good morning!"

Katherine looked up partially startled as she finished signing a high note.

"Good morning Memaw!"

Natalya smiled as she spoke.

"Sounded like a good song. There are scones, muffins, juice and of course tea downstairs if you want. I'm going to call Emily and find out what she would like to do for breakfast."

Katherine walked past Natalya as she looked out the window.

"I'm good actually. Ready for our next adventure."

Katherine sat on the corner of Natalya's bed with her sheepish grin. Natalya scowled as she walked past her and picked up her cell phone. She swallowed as she scanned for Emily's number. She stood up as she pushed the button and waited for the dial tone.

"Good Morning! Yes, we slept very well thank you. I…well yes but…oh…okay. Sure, just let me get a paper and pen."

She motioned to Katherine as she already had the pen and paper to give to her grandmother.

"Okay, go ahead. Yes, I see. Next hill and third driveway. Got it! See you in a few."

Natalya let out a sigh as she brushed the curtains back. Katherine stood up and walked over to her grandmother.

"Something wrong Memaw?"

Katherine saw the mood of her grandmother change.

"No dear. She wants us to have breakfast at her place. It's just that…well… it's suddenly real. All these years, I'm not sure what to expect. Now I'm not sure that this was such a good idea.

She always use to caution me about just give care to the wind and crashing thru things."

Katherine couldn't believe it. Her grandmother seemed to have cold feet in meeting her lost love. She actually smiled and thought it rather sweet. Then her tummy rumbled and she got back to business.

"Come on Memaw. You've come this far. You can't give up now. Besides, she is waiting for you and I want to see your girlfriend!"

Katherine grabbed her grandmothers' arm and gently tugged her towards the door. She picked up the phone keys and wallet on the bed and ushered her Memaw out the room and downstairs to the car.

The English countryside was beautiful and North Yorkshire was no exception. A brief stop for sheep being moved from one pasture to another and they were on their way once again. Suddenly Natalya pulled to the side of a road and got out. Katherine thought she was going to throw up but instead she watched as her grandmother climbed up a hill and across some rocks. She then came back down with a handful of flowers that looked like she just bought them from a flower shop. She watched in amazement as her grandmother poured water on them from their thermos and then wrapped them in The Star newspaper and handed them to Katherine.

"These are absolutely beautiful Memaw. If I hadn't seen where you got them from, I wouldn't have believed it."

Katherine took in their wonderful fragrance as she watched her grandmother.

"Why does it seem that we are the only people out on the road."

Katherine looked both ways to an empty road. He grandmother explained that most of the traffic was in the larger cities. She noticed Katherine looking at the bouquet of flowers as she got in the car.

"They are wildflowers that grow around here mixed with some Heather. I guess I wanted to bring her something."

Katherine patted her grandmother on the arm as they pulled back onto the road. What seemed like a relatively short drive Natalya slowly pulled into the 3rd driveway cautiously checking the address. Katherine noticed her grandmothers breathing increase.

"It'll be alright Memaw. We're almost there!"

There at the end of a winding driveway it opened up as a two-story manor house came in to view. A Land Rover was parked to the side and the barking of a small dog could be heard.

"Wow...Impressive house. I'm assuming it's been in her family?"

All Natalya could seem to do was shake her head as she took the familiar landscape in. The two women got out and Katherine quickly handed her grandmother the freshly picked flowers. They walked up to the door as it opened and a very vocal Corgi came running out.

"Winston! You insulant cur behave yourself."

Katherine knelt down to greet the energetic pup and it immediately rolled over for the familiar belly rubs. As she looked up Natalya stood with flowers in hand as a slightly shorter woman stepped forward. She moved her head to one side as if avoiding Natalya's gaze. Natalya then held out the flowers and as Emily took them Katherine watched as the two women embraced each other. It was as if they were frozen in time. Katherine picked up the Corgi and walked towards Emily. The two women separated and Katherine could see that both had tears in their eyes. Katherine placed the Corgi down as she brushed off her shirt.

"Hi Ms. Winthrop. I'm Katherine...."

Before Katherine could finish her sentence, Emily came over and hugged Katherine.

"Oh yes sweetheart. I know who you are. You're Natalya's beautiful granddaughter. Please forgive Winston's rude behavior. Please! Come in. Breakfast is almost ready."

Emily turned and headed in as the women followed. The entry hall opened up to high ceilings and a wood staircase leading up to a second floor. Katherine looked around as she followed the older women down the side hall and into a slightly smaller brighter room that was the kitchen.

"I thought it might be nice to have breakfast in the garden."

As they walked past the kitchen Katherine could smell bacon and heard the popping up of toast. The other door they went thru opened up to a glass enclosed stone garden and a table decorated with brightly colored dishes. Several covered trays sat to the side on a serving table.

"Please ...sit and make your selves comfortable."

Emily uncovered several trays and began passing plates around full of bacon and sausage, eggs and toast. She then poured tea in each of the cups. Katherine was so hungry the growl of stomach could be heard echoing off the glass.

"Poor dears you must be starving. "

As Katherine stopped focusing on the food, she could see her grandmother focused on Emily. The scarring on her face was mostly hidden by her long grey hair that she had parted to the side. But Katherine knew her grandmother wasn't focusing on Emily's scar. It was as if she was trying to validate what she was seeing. Katherine picked up her fork and started to eat. She was surprised that everything was still warm or hot and very tasty. Winston was back to his well-behaved self as he walked over and curled up in a small dog bed to the side of the breakfast table.

"I'll be right back. I need to put these in water."

She picked up the flowers Natalya had picked for her and disappeared into the kitchen. She then brought out a cobalt blue vase which accentuated the wildflowers and the Heather.

After breakfast Emily gave the women the grand tour of the manor. Lavishly decorated rooms with large balconies were the norm for the 10-room manor. The recent smell of fresh paint was prevalent throughout the manor. Once back downstairs Katherine purposely disappeared into the library. Of all the rooms in the home Katherine found this one the most inviting.

"Well, you can forget about my granddaughter for the next 2 hours!"

Natalya chuckled as Emily laughed.

"Emily, I am so sorry I..."

Emily silenced Natalya with a finger to her lips. It was if a fire ignited within Natalya just from that simple gesture.

"I wasn't sure I could do this. I must have walked a well-defined path in my back yard. The birds weren't much help. But

now that I see you, here, in person, in front of me, I couldn't imagine not doing it."

Natalya pulled Emily closer and embraced her tenderly.

"I know my brother was an ass and I know he manipulated people and you, but he's dead and you are alive! All I want to think about is making up for lost time."

Natalya held her tightly as she spoke.

"You mean after all this time you don't have someone else in your life?"

Emily pushed away slightly as she spoke.

"There never was anyone else. When we were finally rescued from Bataan, I couldn't help but want to regain the reality that was most comforting for me. I sent letters to my brother but the only notice I received was when he told me you had died. I couldn't take it. The treatment of my scars wasn't nearly as painful."

Natalya reached out and brushed the hair away from Emily's face exposing the full effect of the scarring. Emily reached up her hand to stop her but Natalya reached down and gently kissed Emily's lips. She then moved around to gently kiss her scars. Emily relaxed in Natalya's arms.

'Oh Emily...It is I who should apologize for my stubborn and arrogant behavior. Yes, your brother was a horrible man and husband but he gave me a wonderful daughter and I have a beautiful and intelligent granddaughter. If it were not for her, I would have never been reunited with you."

Once again, they kissed. Through all the years and all the difficulties their passion was the one thing that seemed to endure.

It was as if a weight had been lifted from both women. Emily looked up at Natalya and smiled.

"Why don't you and Katherine stay here for the duration of your trip. I certainly have the room and there is even something special I would love to take you to tomorrow. Call it a surprise. What do you say?"

As if she could say anything except yes. Natalya had finally connected with what she believed was her soul mate. From now on she never wanted to let Emily out of her site. Too much time had passed and neither one of them was getting any younger.

"I would love to stay here. I'm sure Katherine would love it too. She eyed your stables on the way in."

Emily walked towards the hallway.

"Does she ride?"

Natalya followed alongside Emily as they went to find Katherine.

"Yes, she does. Her mom has a ranch and she teaches children how to ride both Western and English."

Emily peered into the library where she and Natalya saw Katherine sprawled on the carpet in front of the roaring fireplace reading a book. She turned as she heard the door open wider.

"Hey Memaw...she has some great classic mystery books. Look! Hercule Poirot."

Katherine got up and showed her grandmother the leather-bound gold leafed book. She also noticed her grandmother holding Emily's hand and smiling from ear to ear.

*"How would you like to stay here instead of that inn? Emily
will even give you a tour of the stables."*

Katherine's face lit up as they spoke.

"I'd love it! Are we going now?"

Natalya, not wanting to be separated from Emily, invited her
to come with them as they returned to the inn to gather their
luggage and check out. Emily agreed and made several phone
calls before she left.

As Katherine sat in the back seat of the rover, she noticed
her grandmother holding Emily's hand over the consol. She was
happy for her grandmother. She felt although Emily was a bit shy
still seemed quite nice. Once at the inn Katherine and Natalya
went upstairs to gather their luggage. It wouldn't take long since
neither one really unpacked. Emily spoke with the front desk and
as the two women came back downstairs Natalya noticed people
greeting Emily as if they hadn't seen her in a while. It was then
that Natalya realized that Emily had come out due to her. Emily's
scar had caused her to live alone and her self-imposed exile forced
her to be cut off from neighbors and friends. Each one greeted
her with surprise and commented on how glad they were to see
her out and about.

"I think we have everything."

Natalya interrupted one couple that seemed to want more than
to just say 'Hi'. Emily also seemed a bit uncomfortable as well.

"Oh great! Let's go then. I took care of your bill."

Natalya frowned at Emily paying the bill but she didn't press the
issue since Emily looked like she really wanted to get away from
that couple. Once inside the car Emily explained.

"Ugh! Those were the Tilsdales and they are the towns local gossips. They feel they have to know every detail of why you are in town."

Katherine sat forward and touched Emily's shoulder.

"That's okay. My grandmother will set them straight."

The women laughed as they drove down the road.

"That's what I'm afraid of !"

Emily smiled as she pat Katherine's hand. The ride seemed quicker this time. Maybe it was due to Natalya's knowing the way or maybe it was due to a bit more speed. The women got out while the luggage was squared away. Emily took Katherine over to the stables. There she introduced Katherine to her stable hand Moyra O'Donnell.

"Moyra takes care of the stables and my two geldings Avatar and Star."

Moyra was around Katherine's age and had brilliant green eyes. She smiled as she brought the two saddled horses forward.

"Perhaps Ms. Winthrop you would like me to show Miss Katherine around the grounds."

Emily looked towards Katherine as she climbed up on Star the bay colored Gelding.

"Do you mind dear?"

Emily handed the reins to Moyra.

"That's okay. We will be fine."

Emily winked at Moyra as she headed back to the house.

"Oh! Lunch is at 1:30."

Emily shouted as the two cantered off towards the hills. Emily turned just in time to be greeted by Natalya.

"I think Katherine might have found a friend. Moyra and her are about the same age. Moyra lives at the end of the stables so she's always here."

Natalya looked around briefly and pulled Emily to her and kissed her passionately. Emily liked where that was going so, she pulled away, grabbed Natalya's hand and headed inside the manor. Emily pulled Natalya upstairs to her bedroom. As if not wanting others to interrupt them she closed the door behind them. The aches and pains of an aged body gave way to the gentle and passionate pleasures of touch. Natalya planted gentle kisses on Emily's lips as her hands moved down her shirt to the first button. Emily felt an electrical like charge within her body as Natalya unbuttoned each button. What might have been awkward for some was perfectly natural to Natalya. Gently kissing the nape of Emily's neck as she moved down the front of her cleavage. Emily's breathing increased as Natalya removed her shirt. Emily longed to feel Natalya's skin. She reached down slightly and pulled Natalya's shirt up over her head. Finally, skin to skin was felt. Natalya unsnapped Emily's bra as Emily shuttered. Before Natalya continued, she looked into Emily's face.

"Are you okay?"

Emily reached up and kissed her lips as she answered.

"Never better."

Emily continued to kiss Natalya as she finally removed her bra. Natalya guided Emily to the bed as the two women laid down. Where Natalya's touch was gentle Emily's were passionate and longing. As Natalya's fingers caressed Emily's body they then moved to the button of her jeans. Emily stopped and held Natalya's face in her hands.

"Are you sure about this?"

Emily held Natalya's face awaiting an answer.

"Once again my love you talk too much. I have never been more certain about anything in my life."

With that answer Emily did not hold back. Her need for Natalya was urgent. Natalya herself could feel the heat building within her body. She gave in to Emily with every kiss and every touch. At this point Natalya removed the rest of her clothes as Emily did the same. Each stood briefly as Emily pulled the covers back on her bed. It was as if the wrinkles that time & age placed on their bodies seemed to disappear. Both women climbed in and continued the heat and passion of love making.

Hours later Natalya was awakened by the sound of a song bird outside the window. She looked over at Emily who was sleeping soundly beneath the covers. For the first time since they had met Natalya could now take a good look at the scarring on Emily's face. It ran from the corner of her left eye down her cheek and over to her ear. She continued to trace the scar down the nape of her neck to her shoulder. Natalya could only imagine the pain her beloved must have been in. She continued to gently touch the scar as if trying to heal the pain it must have caused. Suddenly, she noticed Emily's eyes as they focused on her.

"I'm sorry. Did I hurt you? I can't imagine the pain you... I'm so sorry..."

Emily reached up and kissed Natalya to stop her from talking.

"Now who is talking too much?"

Emily smiled as Natalya chuckled. Natalya reached under the covers and pulled Emily to her. The warmth of their bodies touching once again ignited their passion.

Meanwhile, the two younger women raced across the hills down into the pasture and up thru some old ruins. Moyra led Katherine's horse down thru the woods and out towards a clearing that had a brook running across it.

"The horses could use a drink."

She said as she dismounted. Katherine followed and jumped down.

"I could use one too."

As Moyra watched, Katherine knelt down, cupped her hands into the cool, clear water and took a sip.

"You're not a city girl are ye."

Katherine wiped her lips with her sleeve. She thought Moyra had the most beautiful Irish accent she had ever heard.

"Why do you say that?"

Moyra grabbed the reins of the two horses and tied them to an overhanging tree branch. She then sat on one of the larger rocks that overlooked the brook.

"Well, I don't know too many city girls who would drink from a brook let alone wipe their lips with their sleeve."

Katherine looked at Moyra. She reached into her pocket and took out her cell phone. She snapped a photo of an attractive redheaded girl sitting on a rock. She smiled at the picture.

"Whatja do that fer?"

Moyra jumped up not sure what Katherine was doing.

"I just wanted a photo to put in my scrapbook and to show my mum."

Katherine snapped a photograph of the horses drinking and then showed Myra the photos.

"See! Actually, I was raised on a ranch. My mum gives riding lessons to kids. I've been drinking out of creeks, brooks and streams all my life. Going away to college interrupted that. I miss doing stuff like this."

Moyra went back to her rock a bit more at ease.

"What are ya studying in college?"

Katherine sat down in the grass under a tree. She looked up at the clouds as she spoke.

"I was going to be a Psychology major but since visiting my Memaw, ahhh.. grandmother and traveling with her I've developed a love for history and Archeology. My mum would kill me if I changed majors now."

Moyra played with a blade of grass as she spoke.

"But whose doin the studyin? You or your mum?"

Katherine smiled as she looked over at the horses.

"Point taken. I was going to bypass the trauma and just have my grandmother handle my mum."

Moyra checked her watch.

"Ah...I see...you're takin the chicken's way out."

Katherine saw that Moyra was checking the time. She reached up and handed the reins of Moyra's horse to her as she climbed aboard hers.

"Yah...pretty much."

With that , the two riders were on their way back to the manor for lunch.

Meanwhile, back at the manor house Emily was changing her clothes as she looked over at Natalya's silhouette under the covers. Natalya was even more content than Emily remembered after their sessions of lovemaking.

"Come on sleepy head. Its almost lunch time and I've got to get down to the kitchen to prepare it. Come on!"

Emily threw Natalya's clothes to her as she picked them up off the floor.

"The bathroom is thru there and I will expect you down in the kitchen shortly."

She had a wicked grin as she blew Natalya a kiss and hurried out the door. Natalya got dressed, freshened up and hurried down the stairs.

Emily was busy laying out sandwiches and soup as the two girls walked in the kitchen door that led to the outside.

"I hope you don't mind. I invited Moyra to come eat with us."

Moyra smiled politely as she followed Katherine. Natalya was glad to see that Katherine had a friend. She was worried about part of the trip being boring for 28 year old granddaughter. But she watched as the two made eye contact and quietly spoke to one another.

Emily motioned for everyone to sit down. As dishes clanked and conversations continued Emily wanted to take Natalya to a particular event that she wanted to surprise her with. Katherine wondered if she could explore the town on the way. Moyra suggested that she could take her and show her the town while Emily went with Natalya. They could then meet back here for a late dinner. Natalya watched as Katherine lit up at that suggestion. She looked over at Emily, winked and said it sounded like a plan. After lunch everyone helped with the dishes and shortly after that the women loaded up into the car. As Emily drove towards town she would point out sites of interest and spoke of how Harrowgate grew out of two smaller settlements. She also mentioned the towns spa water contains iron, Sulphur and salt.

"Most people commute that work in Leeds, Bradford and York area. Our shopping district incorporates Cambridge Street, Oxford Street. But the boutique shops are nicer on Parliament Street and in the Montpellier Quarter."

She looked in her rear view mirror as she spoke. The girls seemed to light up at the shopping prospects. The girls were dropped off at the edge of town and Moyra assured the women that they would catch a ride home either on one of the busses or her brothers trolley. After about a half an hour a field came in to view. Cars were parked to one side of a field as people walked over the hill. Once Emily & Natalya crested the hill Natalya could see what Emily's surprise was.

Planes were on one side of the field across from an airstrip. An assortment of planes could be readily seen.

"Surprise!"

Natalya reached over and kissed Emily on the cheek. As they got out of the rover Emily brushed her hair to the side of her scar and pulled out a rather large hat & scarf. Natalya realized that was Emily's comfort zone and said nothing. They paid the entry fee and started to walk around. Emily could see that Natalya was like a child in a candy shop. The airshow had its usual popular crowd. Natalya was being very attentive to Emily as she asked questions about various planes and their features. It was like having a private tour. Emily was getting thirsty and told Natalya that she would meet her over by the last section of planes. Natalya started to object but Emily winked at her and for the first time that day had touched her arm in public. Emily went thru the gauntlet of sellers till she came to the drink stand. She waited behind several teenagers as she tilted her head slightly with her large hat. With her hair partially combed to one side her scars were barely visible. She watched as Natalya was in her element. Natalya smiled as she walked past the planes from all over the world. This aviation fair drew planes from WWII to the present. She marveled at the extreme care some of the planes were given. As she stood beside the B-17 she felt a gentle tap on her shoulder. She turned to be greeted by a much older wrinkled woman.

"I thought that might be you Captain Ritenkoph."

The older woman shook Natalya's hand firmly as she smiled. Suddenly, when the woman smiled Natalya remembered the woman from her past. A woman who always made sure Natalya's plane was fit to fly. It was her old mechanic from back in the day when she flew Po-2's. Natalya pulled the woman closer and hugged her.

"Inna you old goat! How are you?"

The mechanic turned to point to the planes.

"Isn't this glorious? To see all these planes in one spot."

Natalya smiled as she followed her friend. They walked past planes from their past like the P-38's, P-51's and AT-6's.

"Look! They even have some Russian planes."

The women fondly touched the tail fins of the Yak-1b and the huge Petlyakov PE-2 bomber.

"That is why they asked me here. After the war I bought some of the surviving PO-2's. Ugh...they were is such horrible shape. I salvaged what I could to build 3 beautiful PO-2's."

As Inna finished her sentence, she steered Natalya around the Russian bomber till one small yellow and grey camouflaged plane could be seen. Natalya's eyes began to tear. She walked slowly over to the tiny bi-plane taking in every inch of her body. She caressed the planes body sensually as Inna smiled.

"Oh, Inna ...she is truly beautiful!"

Inna stood in front of her friend beaming. She knew if anyone could appreciate her reconstruction Natalya the pilot could.

"Would you like to take her for a spin?"

She turned and looked at Inna like a kid in a candy store that was just told they could have anything in the store they wanted.

"Oh Inna. I don't know...I "

Inna pulled Natalya up onto the steps that made the viewing of the cockpits of certain planes easier to see.

"See! Just as you remembered just with a bit better engine modification. She now has an electric start and communications!"

Natalya could not stop smiling. She went all around the plane with her eyes as she grasped the edges of the cockpit.

"Inna ...are you sure?"

Inna reached into a box behind the steps and pulled out an old bomber jacket and goggles.

" I just happen to have two."

Natalya grabbed the jacket and goggles and headed for the co-pilots seat which in these bi-planes was up in front.

"No here! You fly her."

Natalya slid into the pilot's seat. She figured if she couldn't handle it her friend would be able to take over the controls. While Inna's young assistant came over ready to wind the propeller Inna waved him away.

"One of the modifications I told you about...electric start."

The plane started up at the push of a button. Natalya taxied to a prepared runway while people started to look on. Inna had also installed radio communications and was given clearance to take off . The PO-2 needed very little runway making them great short take off planes. Halfway down the runway she took off. Natalya banked and was able to fly at a lower altitude than other heavier planes. She flew above the fair with its neatly arranged planes. She suddenly realized she needed a special someone to share this moment with. She flew back to the runway but really didn't need it due to the large empty field next to them.

"Inna, I have a favor to ask of you."

Natalya climbed carefully out of the cockpit and used the footpads on the wing to hop down. She cleared her favor with Inna and went to find Emily but to her amazement there standing under the wing of the Yak-1 fighter was Emily. She looked down at the ground and forced a smile as she looked up at Natalya.

"I thought I might find you here. Want a sip?"

Emily offered Natalya a sip of her soda. As Natalya accepted, she held Emily's arm as they walked towards the PO-2.

"Come! Now you can finally get a feel for the old girl."

As Natalya put her drink down Inna removed her bomber jacket and helped Emily put it on.

"Oh, by the way ...that is Inna my mechanic from the war."

Emily felt a bit confused but smiled at the woman's introduction as she was guided by her to climb up into the plane. Emily turned to Inna and asked…

"Are you sure this is okay? I mean I wouldn't want to sit and ruin your seats."

Both women laughed out loud as Emily was guided into the co-pilot's cockpit. Natalya shook Inna's hand as she climbed into the pilot's seat. Emily looked around at the narrowness of the cockpit and how exposed one was.

"Isn't this great!"

Natalya was in her element.

"Yes, it's certainly interesting."

Suddenly Natalya shouted…

"Do you trust me?"

Emily thought Natalya was being her usual silly self.

"Of course, I trust you…but why?"

Suddenly, the engine started and Natalya was speaking into her radio headset. The plane began to taxi towards the runway as Emily's heart began to race. She started to hold on to her hat and then thought better of it and removed it.

"What are you doing? Natalya!"

Emily realized too late what Natalya meant by 'trust'. She thought Natalya simply wanted her to sit in the plane she use to fly. She was too stunned to speak as the plane rose magically in the air. Due to the fact that the PO-2's were not terribly fast Emily viewed her countryside from a whole new perspective. She marveled at the greenery and the hills. She could feel the coolness of the air but felt quite cozy in the bomber jacket she was given. Natalya flew close enough to the clouds that Emily felt she could touch them. As she glided over the water Emily finally understood Natalya's love for flying. The war was so long ago and the images of the horror had long since faded. Emily also realized how truly vulnerable Natalya was in this plane. With bombs dropping, machine guns firing in a canvas and wood plane she had a whole new appreciation for Natalya's side of the war. She was very lucky that Natalya had returned to her.

As Natalya landed the plane back by the steps Inna came running over. She held a tablet in her hand and handed it and a keyring to Natalya.

"You better take off. The organizers aren't happy that I let you fly her. Everything you need is on that pad. Don't worry. It's okay……now go!"

Natalya threw Inna Emily's car keys and turned the plane. Inna headed towards a group of 4 stern old men as they marched past the other planes with definite determination. Natalya grabbed the stick of the plane as she taxied once more to the runway waiting for clearance. Once the clearance was given they were up in the air once more. Emily decided to get into character and put the headset on that was laying by her feet.

"So what now? Are we fugitives? Are we going to get shot out of the air? If so, I have already done that. Have the scars to prove it."

Natalya was smiling as she read the tablet and looked over the side of the plane at the ground for reference.

"I can assure you my love that we will not be shot down... at least not yet."

Emily felt a warmth come over her. Natalya had not referred to her as "My love" since the war. A more private yet medium sized airport was coming into view. Natalya banked and told Emily to hold on. The wind had shifted a bit but Natalya handled it with very little problem. Her landing was perfect and surprisingly smooth at least for Emily. She taxied to a blue and gold hanger and removed her headset once they were in the hanger. She waited for Emily to stand up and start to climb down so she could help her.

Once on the ground Emily stopped Natalya, cupped her face in between her hands and kissed her passionately. Natalya responded and pulled Emily closer.

"What was that for?"

Natalya asked as Emily rested her head on her shoulder covering her scarred side of her face.

"I now understand your love of flying although I'm not sure I like the type of plane you flew. I'm not sure what my brother was thinking and I don't want to go there right now. At this moment, here, right now I am glad you lived and I'm glad that you reached out and found me."

Natalya hugged her tightly, kissed her lips and brushed away the hair from the side of her face that exposed her scars. Emily reached up to stop her hand but Natalya kissed her gently again.

"I finally want to see all of you . I feel like I have waited so long to finally find you and I don't want to live the rest of my life without you. I..."

Natalya motioned for Emily to stay where she was as Natalya climbed over to the plane to remove the keys Inna had given her. She untwisted a small ringlet from the keyring and went back to Emily who stood watching her. She came over and slowly knelt down on one knee.

"Please forgive the design as it were but Emily Gayle Winthrop would you kindly accept my proposal to be my wife?"

Natalya placed the tiny ringlet over Emily's finger as she proposed. Emily looked down at her with a smirk. She then reached down and pulled Natalya towards her.

"I would be truly honored. Of course, I'll marry you!"

The two women embraced for what seemed like hours.

"I think it's time we went, home, don't you?"

Emily looked around as the sun was beginning to drop below the trees.

" I think that is an excellent idea. But we will have to wait at the inn, give Inna back her car keys so we can get your rover and collect OUR granddaughter."

Natalya looked around for a car that fit the keys insignia. A fairly new 2 door black Jaguar sat quietly in a corner.

" Humm…remind me to speak with Inna about her choice of cars."

Emily followed Natalya.

"Why what is it? Oh, my lord…."

Just as Emily followed Natalya, she could see what car she was talking about.

"Well looks like the drive to the inn is going to be as fun as the flight!"

"I can think of worst ways than riding off towards the sunset in a convertible Jaguar."

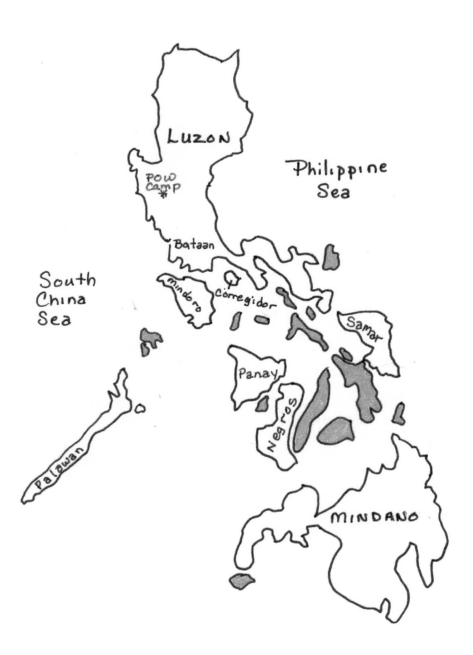

Philippines

Unknown officer, General Patton,
General Arnold and Unknown Officer.

My mother, Irene Levy Haspiel
on her way to work at the Pentagon.

BIBLIOGRAPHY

Farrell, Mary Cronk *Pure Grit: How American World War II Nurses Survived Battle and Prison Camp in the Pacific*. Abrams Books for Young Readers, 2014

Norman, Elizabeth M. *We Band of Angels: The Untold Story of American Nurses Trapped on Bataan By the Japanese.* New York, Pocket Books, 1999

Macadam, Heather Dune *999: The Extraordinary Young Women of the First Official Jewish Transport to Auschwitz*. Kensington Publishing Corp. 2020

Smimova-Medvedeva, Zoia Mateevna. *On the Road to Stalingrad: Memoirs of a Woman Machine Gunner*. New Military Publishing, 1997

Pearson, P. O'Connell, *Fly Girls: The Daring Women Pilots Who Helped Win WWII.* Simon & Schuster, 2018

Mundy, Liza *Code Girls: The Untold Story of the American Women Codebreakers of World War II.* Hachette Books, 2017

Cole, Jean Hascall, *Women Pilots of World War II.* University of Utah Press, 1992

Berube, Allan, *Coming Out Under Fire: The History of Gay Men and Women in World War II,* Simon & Schuster, 1990